EDUCATOR'S GUIDE TO
Mission in Practice

DISCIPLESHIP IN ACTION IN CATHOLIC SCHOOLS

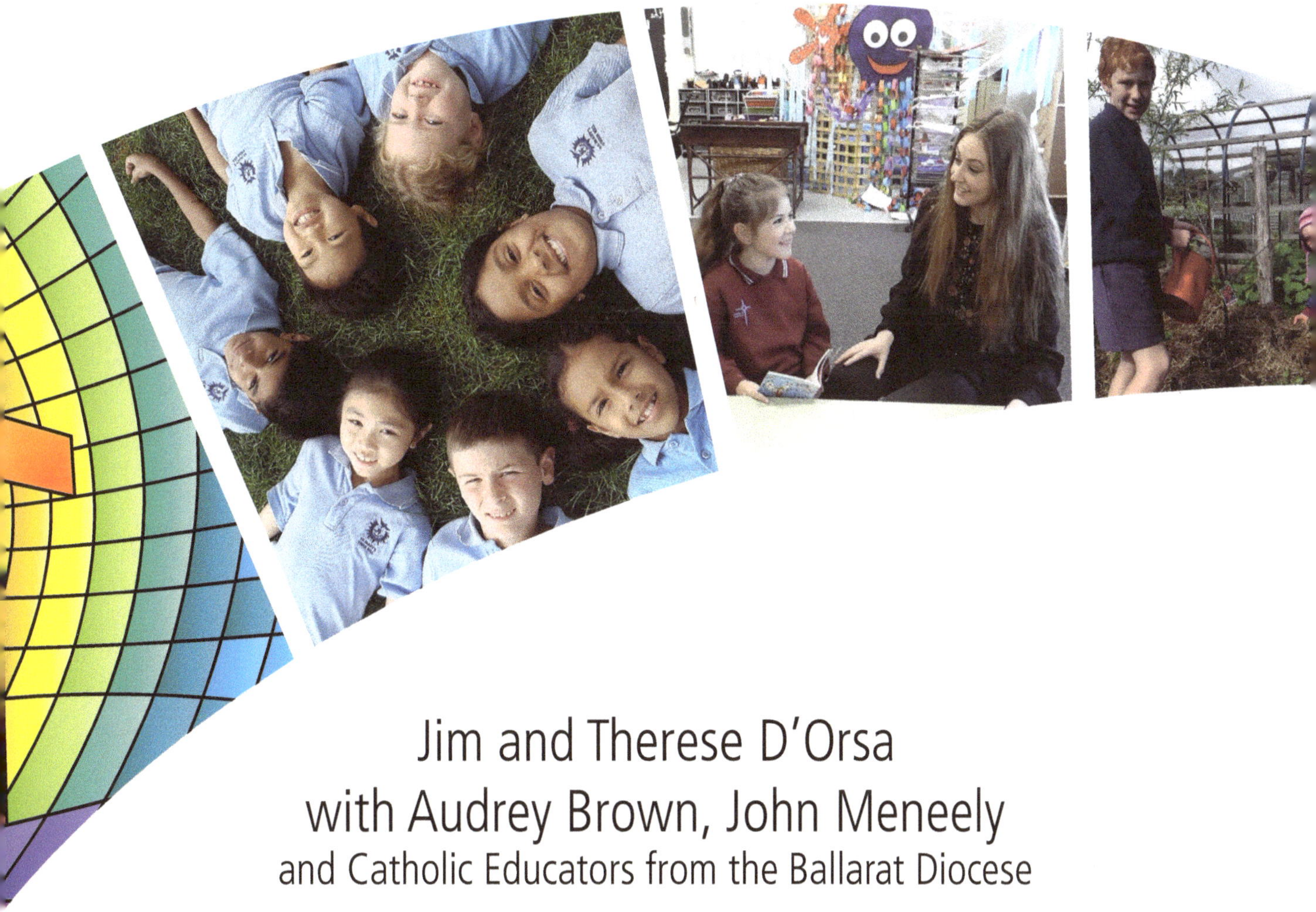

Jim and Therese D'Orsa
with Audrey Brown, John Meneely
and Catholic Educators from the Ballarat Diocese

The *Educator's Guides*

The Mission and Education Project of BBI-TAITE (The Australian Institute of Theological Education) presents a series of Guides to serve the educational mission of Catholic schools in Australia and beyond. The Guides, each dealing with a specific area, introduce educators to ways in which mission and education may be integrated in the life and work of Catholic educators and students. The mandate given to the expert writers who create these Guides is to tap into the best available treatments of mission and also to ground their work in quality practice.

Therese D'Orsa
Professor Mission and Culture
BBI-TAITE
Commissioning Editor Mission and Education Project

Published in Australia by Vaughan Publishing
32 Glenvale Crescent, Mulgrave VIC 3170

A joint imprint of Garratt Publishing and BBI – The Australian Institute of Theological Education.

Copyright © 2019 Jim & Therese D'Orsa

All rights reserved. Except as provided by Australian copyright law, no part of this publication may be reproduced in any manner without prior permission in writing from the publisher.

Cover design and typesetting by Marley Berger
Images supplied by All Saints Catholic School Portland, the Catholic Communities of the Hampden Region, St Francis Xavier Ballarat, St Patrick's College Ballarat, St Mary's Swan Hill, St Patrick's School Port Fairy, St Patrick's Stawell, St Alipius Ballarat East, Columban Centre for Christian-Muslim Relations
Printed by Tingleman

The author and publisher gratefully acknowledge the permission granted to reproduce the copyright material in this book. Every effort has been made to trace copyright holders and to obtain their permission for the use of copyright material.

The publisher apologises for any errors or omissions in the above list and would be grateful if notified of any corrections that should be incorporated in future reprints or editions of this book.

ISBN 9780648524601

 A catalogue record for this book is available from the National Library of Australia

Nihil Obstat: Reverend Monsignor Gerard J Diamond STD
Diocesan Censor
Imprimatur: Monsignor Greg Bennet MS STL VG
Vicar General
Date: 30 April 2019

The *Nihil Obstat* and *Imprimatur* are official declarations that a book or pamphlet is free of doctrinal or moral error. No implication is contained therein that those who have granted the *Nihil Obstat* and *Imprimatur* agree with the contents, opinions or statements expressed. They do not necessarily signify that the work is approved as a basic text for catechetical instruction.

Contents

Introduction		1
Chapter 1	Mission and God's Kingdom	3
Chapter 2	Forming Disciples for the Kingdom	7
Chapter 3	Mission and Identity – Catholic Does as Catholic Is	11
Chapter 4	Biblical Traditions of Mission	16
Chapter 5	Catholic Schools – Mission Within a Worldwide Family	23
Chapter 6	Mapping Mission Across Time	28
Chapter 7	Mission Between Peoples – an Unfolding Tradition	36
Chapter 8	Dialogue – a Vital Mode of Mission	40
Chapter 9	Mission – the Task of the Whole Community	46
Chapter 10	Theological Reflection for Mission	51
Conclusion	God's Mission Has a Faith Community	56
Prayer		57
Endnotes		58
Further Reading		60

Meet the Authors

Jim D'Orsa

Jim D'Orsa's contributions to Catholic education include teaching and senior leadership in Catholic schools and systems. He pioneered the preparation of lay leaders to take responsibility for the vision and mission of colleges, and has extensive experience in reviewing large systems and in pastoral planning. Jim is currently associate professor at BBI-TAITE where he specialises in teaching, research and writing in the areas of mission, leadership and theology.

Therese D'Orsa

Therese D'Orsa is currently professor of mission and culture at BBI-TAITE. She has a long experience of leadership in schools and school systems, and in adult education, and has taught in a range of tertiary institutions, both universities and theologates. Therese has led major projects in mission, education and justice. She has written widely on mission and education and has pioneered the Mission and Education project of which she is the Commissioning Editor.

Audrey Brown

Audrey Brown has been Director of Catholic Education for the Diocese of Ballarat since 2012. She has been a teacher, teacher coach, principal and principal coach, all in regional Victoria. A lifelong learner who has engaged in study and research throughout her career, Audrey has post-graduate qualifications in educational leadership, Religious Education, theology, education law and educational system leadership.

John Meneely

John is currently Deputy Director of Catholic Education in the Diocese of Ballarat. He has extensive experience in faith leadership at both school and system level. John has a passion for religious education that is reflective of the authentic dialogue between faith and culture and has been involved in curriculum development in this field for fifteen years.

Audrey Brown and John Meneely worked collaboratively with educators from across the Ballarat Diocese for this book.

Introduction
Mission in Practice in Catholic Schools

As the renewal inaugurated by the Second Vatican Council (1962–5) has taken root in the life of the Catholic community worldwide, the mission of Jesus has come more clearly into focus as the wellspring and raison d'être of its life.

It is also now clearer that strains and fractures in key human relationships must cause mission to take many new forms, and that familiar forms of mission must morph into new configurations. Justice, peace-making, reconciliation, care for the earth, and the ongoing challenge of inculturating the Gospel deeply into the cultures of each human grouping, are clear examples of forms of mission which are central to keeping hope alive in our time.

Vatican II inaugurated a paradigm shift in understanding about mission, moving God's action in the created world to the centre of mission theology and practice, and acknowledging the Church's vital role in the service of a mission which is, first and foremost, God's project. The Church is a community intentionally at the service of God's mission.

In recent decades, the Church community has come to understand more clearly Jesus' teaching about the Kingdom of God. In this perspective, God is the one who is in control of mission; the Church – every community and each of the baptised – has a vocation of collaboration in making present and sustaining the Kingdom of God. Jesus' ministry of teaching and healing provides the example of mission in practice. As faith communities gathered by the Church for the ministry of education, Catholic schools are privileged partners in the work of God's Kingdom.

The current context of mission, with its rapid globalisation, pluralism, and maelstrom of ideologies and philosophical currents impacting on the human community and the natural world, is substantially different from that of the times of Vatican II. In the light of the contemporary challenges, BBI-TAITE (The Australian Institute of Theological Education) has entered into a partnership with a number of educational providers to initiate a series of explorations and conversations set at the interface of mission and education. These take the form of Exploratory Studies, Educator's Guides, and Monographs. In this Educator's Guide, Catholic educators from the schools and the Catholic Education Office of the Ballarat diocese, have worked with missiologists Jim and Therese D'Orsa, to provide an introduction to 'mission in practice' in order to support Catholic school communities in recognising the many opportunities they have for addressing contemporary mission challenges.

The Mission and Education Project is national, not only in seeking, and gratefully receiving, financial support from many diocesan and congregational school systems, but also in drawing as many educators as possible into the conversation. My sincere thanks to all those Catholic educational authorities who have supported this project over the past decade.

As Commissioning Editor, I take the opportunity to acknowledge the generosity and optimism of the Ballarat educators who assisted in the development of this Guide. The Director, Audrey Brown, and Deputy Director, John Meneely, worked with the skill and energy of true leaders to engage with school communities and prepare the eight case studies that emerged out of their conversations with school staffs. These case studies have been placed throughout the text. I feel sure that every Catholic educator in and beyond Australia will find they can recognise similar good practice occurring in their own dioceses and schools. This Guide is a call to affirm and celebrate good mission practice, and to go deeper in faith, spirituality and competence.

It can be a challenge to conceptualize and express clearly what we know intuitively about the many forms that mission takes today. My hope is that this Guide will help Catholic educators and leaders to do just that. In the unfolding story of God's mission, we are co-creators. We are also educators, and it is important that we are clear in our own understanding, and can explain mission to others.

Mission's scriptural foundations, touched on in this Guide (chapters 1 and 4), teach us much about the 'three steps forwards and two steps backwards' that mission entails. Our own experience provides us with similar insight on this score. We know that endeavoring to create and sustain kingdom times and spaces in our communities and contexts, is a 'long haul process'.

Pope Francis has issued a call for Catholic communities to form 'missionary disciples'. Such formation occurs in the process of engagement in mission practice, in deep reflection, and in respectful dialogue. Mission in Practice is offered to those entrusted with the ongoing formation of educators, in the hope that it may enable them to see contours of mission a little more clearly, so that as educators they may be confident in their missional vocations. Amid much brokenness, mission work engenders hope.

Educators who bring hope to others *must also be sustained in hope themselves*. In the words of one of the great mission texts of our time, may this Guide encourage and enable those who study it, to: 'Always be ready to make your defense to anyone who demands from you an accounting for the hope that is within you; yet do it with gentleness and reverence.' (1 Peter 3:15)

The Guide begins by outlining core understandings about mission in the context of Catholic schooling, drawing particularly on the teaching of Pope Francis (Chapters 1-3). It then goes on to outline the scriptural foundations on which the theology of mission rests (Chapter 4) and the way in which this relates to the Church's official understanding of Catholic education and its mission to students (Chapter 5). This understanding has sometimes struggled to keep pace with developments in mission theology.

In Chapters 6, 7, and 8 the Guide traces developments in the Church community's understanding and experience of mission as these have evolved across two millennia. These chapters make the point that God's mission can take many forms each of which is related to the needs of people. As historical and cultural contexts unfold needs change and so too, in response, does our understanding of mission.

While mission may take the many forms outlined in the Guide, it always involves three fundamental modes; *witness* to the message of the Gospel; *proclamation* of the message of the Gospel; *dialogue* with others seeking their engagement in action on behalf of the needy and marginalised.

Mission has an essential *communal dimension* as it is the work of a community rather than of individuals (Chapter 9). Mission is also an *inclusive concept* in that all members of a school community have the talent needed to contribute in creating 'Kingdom spaces' in students' lives. The various examples drawn from the Ballarat schools make this clear.

The method of theological reflection presented in this Guide (Chapter 10) provides a way of processing life experiences in all their complexity to identify and meet human needs. The final chapter outlines a method of reflection that has a long provenance in the development of Catholic Social Teaching and the praxis of social action on behalf of the marginalised. It provides a general framework for working through issues thrown up by the reflections presented in the text.

Therese D'Orsa
Professor Mission and Culture,
Broken Bay Institute
Commissioning Editor

Always be ready to make your defense to anyone who demands from you an accounting for the hope that is in you; yet do it with gentleness and reverence.

1 Peter 3:15

CHAPTER 1

Mission and God's Kingdom

The Kingdom of God is not a concept, a doctrine, or a program subject to free interpretation, but is before all else, a person with the face and name of Jesus of Nazareth, the image of the invisible God. (Pope John Paul II Redemptoris Missio *# 18).*

Sometimes we hear people use expressions like: 'I'm on a mission to sort this out.' In the broader culture, 'mission' equates with purpose or direction, implying a desire to achieve something important.

In the language and culture of Catholicism, 'mission' equates to our faith community's religious purpose, its raison d'être, which is to be intentionally at the service of God's Kingdom, in our personal lives, and in communities, societies, and cultures. This is the sense in which we use 'mission' in this Guide.

We explore ways in which school communities understand and carry out the mission of Jesus in settings very different from those in which Jesus pursued his mission from God, to whom he related as Father. When Jesus spoke about his mission, he used a phrase that touched into the culture of the people to whom he was speaking. He referred to 'the kingdom (or reign) of God', in other words, 'what things would be like around here for people if God's wishes and intentions were making the running'.

The Kingdom of God and the reign or rule of God are synonyms. Sometimes people express this as God's dream for creation – an appropriate way of fostering understanding of Jesus' image for his mission.

In making the idea of the 'Kingdom of God' concrete for people, Jesus used images and parables. These often indicated that the Kingdom of God is different from what people first imagine, is very valuable, and comes at a high price for his followers.

> The kingdom of heaven is like a merchant searching for fine pearls. When he finds a pearl of great price, he goes and sells all that he has and buys it. (Matt 13:45-46).[1]

Choices have to be made, and considerable effort exerted, in order for the Kingdom of God to break into the tangle of human relationships.

Engagement with the Marginalised

Jesus' teaching and healing ministries were directed at all who were open to receive the gift God was offering. Those on the margins of society were in great need of the healing and dignity that Jesus afforded them. For this reason, Jesus offered them particular attention. For all who were prepared to listen and follow him as disciples, Jesus showed that they were to authenticate their relationship with God by making choices similar to those that he was making. Effectively, Jesus was calling for a new form of human consciousness – the capacity to view things differently, to imagine a better situation and then make it happen.

Jesus' followers (disciples) were called to create 'kingdom times and spaces' wherever they encountered people in need, or any of the key human relationships – with God, self, others or the natural world – under stress.

The Kingdom is in the Process

Many of the kingdom images used by Jesus involve what we might term 'process' words – he spoke, for example, of a woman *searching* for a lost coin (Luke 15:8-10), a farmer *sowing* seed (Matt 13:1-9), a king *preparing* a wedding feast (Matt 22:1-14), yeast silently *leavening* the dough (Matt 13:33). The Kingdom of God requires serious work. It is present in the efforts to create 'kingdom spaces' in areas of life where the values of the Kingdom are absent. The Kingdom is present as much in the *process* of endeavouring to bring it about as in the *outcome*.

While already among us (Luke 17:21), the Kingdom is never complete in this world, no matter how great our efforts or noteworthy our successes. That is why Jesus taught us to pray for the coming of the Kingdom in the prayer we know as the Our Father – 'Your kingdom come, your will be done, on earth as in heaven'.

Splendid gains are sometimes made, but that is not the end of it. There is always a continuing, or a new, challenge to be faced. This is because of the tendency for human arrangements to deteriorate, even when they are well established. Eventually renewal will be necessary.

Consequently, there is no justification for the disciple to rest on her laurels, to bask in mission accomplished. In this world, our achievements on behalf of the Kingdom are *always provisional, and only ever partially complete*.

Jesus Embodies the Kingdom

In his magisterial treatment of the Kingdom of God,[2] Pope John Paul II reminded us that Jesus reveals the characteristics of the kingdom through his words, his actions, and his person. Jesus is the kingdom made visible.

> The Kingdom of God is not a concept, a doctrine, or a program subject to free interpretation, but is before all else, a person with the face and name of Jesus of Nazareth, the image of the invisible God. (*Redemptoris Missio* # 18).

Jesus proclaimed the Good News by totally identifying with what he was announcing – in him words were perfectly matched with deeds. We might say today that 'he walked the talk'.

As a result of his choices, he was to experience personally the price of living the values, responsibilities, and relationships of the Kingdom in daily life: conflict, bitter suffering and even death.

However, the Kingdom of God ultimately includes overcoming death. The Kingdom reaches its completion beyond this world and beyond time. When Paul and the Gospel writers wanted to present the Good News after Jesus had sent the Holy Spirit, they proclaimed the totality of what the Good News entails – always telling the *full story* of Jesus – his life, mission, message, death and resurrection.

A Change of Mind and Heart

Pope John Paul II emphasised the change of mind and heart, and allegiance to Jesus (faith), which goes with acceptance of the good news of God's reign or kingdom.

This change of mind and heart is part and parcel of discipleship of Jesus.

> This is the time of fulfilment. The kingdom of God is at hand. Repent, and believe in the gospel. (Mk 1:15).

A change of mind and heart (sometimes termed 'conversion' or 'repentance') and the allegiance to Jesus which is its expression, transform all relationships – with God, self, others, and the natural world.

Jesus Formed a Community for Mission

Much of Jesus' effort in his short public life went into forming a community of disciples for the Kingdom. Following his resurrection and the sending of the Holy Spirit, these early followers were to go into the known world and participate in the Kingdom process just as Jesus had done. Most paid a similar price to Jesus in their service of the Kingdom of God.

Pope Francis has described the Church as a 'community of missionary disciples' (*The Joy of the Gospel* ##119-121).[3] The forming and sustaining of such communities is the responsibility of all who lead in Catholic schools, and also of each community member – all are called to contribute to the strength and viability of missional communities.

Mission and Evangelisation

These are closely related concepts, sometimes used interchangeably. In simple terms, the relationship is as follows: the mission (religious purpose) of the Christian community comes from God, and it is to evangelise i.e. to make present, by deed and word, the Good News of God's kingdom as Jesus did. Service on behalf of this kingdom of love, justice, peace, mercy and reconciliation is the raison d'être of the community we call Church.

The phrase 'new evangelisation' should not be taken to mean some kind of new, in the sense of different, understanding of the community's fundamental mission. The phrase refers simply to the call to Catholics (first issued by Pope John Paul II) to renew their enthusiasm, and expand their capacities, for bringing the Good News *in all its many forms* to bear on the lives, communities and cultures of humans in the contemporary world.

Linking the Concepts[4]

God's Mission	**God's mission** to the world – what God is effecting.
Jesus' Mission	**Jesus' mission** – to be and to proclaim the good news of God's kingdom.
Church's Mission	**Our mission as Disciples** – to learn from Jesus and to continue his mission to make God's kingdom present in our world.

Reflection

In this Guide we endeavour to translate Jesus' teaching about the kingdom or rule of God into the idea of 'kingdom spaces' i.e. 'spaces' in school life where members of the community experience justice, reconciliation, peace and love, often in the form of compassion. All are hallmarks of God's kingdom breaking into human experience in concrete ways. While it is important to create such 'spaces' for all students, it is especially important to create them for those who are marginalised.

1. Reflect on your interactions with students and see if you can identify such experiences.

2. Who are the marginalised in your school, or class? What do you think a 'kingdom space' might look like for these students? How would you go about creating these? Be as specific as you can. Remember, mission always happens in the concrete, never in the abstract.

Proclamation of the Gospel as an Invitation to Prayer
All Saints Catholic School, Portland

With a diverse faith background of families and staff, All Saints Catholic School in Portland, Victoria, decided to create a prayer experience that was open and respectful of all members of the school community. Using funds and volunteer labour offered by Portland Aluminium, the school leadership decided to build a walking labyrinth that would provide a space and opportunity for prayer and reflection.

The school had taught students a range of meditative practices which provided the grounding to introduce the labyrinth. Labyrinth walking does not presume a familiarity with the words and language of prayer but leads the seeker to an encounter. Ironically, proclamation of the Gospel, which may seem to some to be very much about words, does not necessarily come in the form of the spoken or written word, but as this community found, it can come very effectively through an invitation to silence, stillness and simplicity.

One way in which the labyrinth has been used by both students and staff is as a form of centring prayer prompted by a passage of scripture that could be used as a focus if so desired by the participant. An important element of this tactile prayer is the feeling of pebbles underfoot that connects the participant with God's earth through touch and sound.

Plans are afoot to extend an invitation to the parent body and parishioners to learn about, and participate in, labyrinth prayer, thus strengthening partnerships in the education of faith. This provides an important opportunity to bear witness to the invitation of Jesus to his followers, to 'Come and See'. (John 1:39)

CHAPTER 2
Forming Disciples for the Kingdom

Every Christian is a missionary to the extent that he or she has encountered the love of God in Christ Jesus: we no longer say that we are 'disciples' and 'missionaries', but rather that we are always 'missionary disciples'. Pope Francis (*The Joy of the Gospel* #120)

In this chapter we will take time to look more specifically at the call to discipleship as we learn about this from the Gospels. We will consider the implications for each person, and for leaders who hold designated responsibility for missional formation, that is for the forming of communities of missionary disciples. We will acknowledge discipleship as *vocation*, i.e. a call to *relationship with Jesus, and to a sharing of his mission*.

As we see from the Gospels, disciple-making requires *learning on the job, times of instruction, and a praxis approach, that is an ongoing cycle of action and reflection*. Christian praxis involves both involvement in mission and reflection on that involvement in the light of faith. Christian reflection is a combination of deep thought and prayer. The vocation to missionary discipleship is lived out in the community, and indeed, as Pope Francis reminds us, the whole Church is called collectively as well as individually to missionary discipleship (c.f. *The Joy of the Gospel* #40).

Nothing is more immediate, demanding, and enlightening to those entrusted with the work of disciple-making than a close reading of the Gospels in order to familiarise oneself with how Jesus formed his disciples. Indeed much of what we know of Jesus comes to us through the Gospel accounts of Jesus' relationships with his chosen followers, both the broader group of disciples and the twelve apostles who symbolised the scattered house of Israel. Jesus saw it as his mission to restore the house of Israel, not politically in a direct sense, but through the service of teaching and healing directed in a special way to the marginalised – that is, he was restoring the spirit of the Exodus covenant. There were enormous political consequences, however, as Jesus' ministry was deeply challenging to Israel's rulers, who colluded with the Romans to crucify him.

Like every human being, Jesus formed his identity through his relationships – with the one he called Abba (father), with family, friends, others in his society, and with the natural world as experienced in his home country of Israel.

When we read the gospels, we are accessing sources that were written some decades after Jesus' death and resurrection, and the sending of the Holy Spirit. In doing so, we have the advantage of listening closely to the struggles of real communities who were trying to form missionary disciples in the light of Jesus' experiences and their own experiences of doing so.

In the gospels, the story of Jesus is told in such a way as to make sense of their struggles as communities lived out their lives of faith in a demanding environment, one in which many different belief systems swirled, and in which their own faith was not much appreciated nor understood.

Discipleship as Vocation

The story form in which the gospels were written is a dynamic medium that invites the reader into the action. This means that we are considering the gospel account not only in terms of the original life of Jesus and his disciples, and not only in terms of the issues affecting the communities out of which the Gospels came, *but also in terms of the needs of our Christian communities in the twenty-first century.*

All four gospels have a strong focus on Jesus' formative relationship with his disciples. He called them to follow him as he moved with compassion among the people. Read the stories of the call to discipleship – Mark 1:16–20; Matt 4:18–20; Luke 5:1–11. In John's Gospel (John 1:39–41), the portrayal is one of a compelling force attracting disciples to Jesus. The fact that we have stories of disciples being formed into a community of followers in all four gospels indicates a strong call tradition held within the Christian communities at the time.[5]

The gathering of disciples around an expert in Jewish law was common practice at the time, but the norm was for disciples to choose a master whom they would ask to teach them in matters of the law; in the case of Jesus it is the master who calls and selects. The most unlikely people in terms of occupation and personality are called – fishermen, tax collectors, and those described as 'hotheads' (sons of thunder). Discipleship today is no different. The whole range of human characters are called to discipleship. All, with their many gifts and shortcomings, are the concern of leaders of Christian communities such as schools, parishes, and health care services.

The call to discipleship is unequivocal and demanding and the old way of living must be left behind, along with the old securities. Although it is likely that the process of attaching to Jesus took longer than the literary form and style of the Gospels allows for, the demand for a radical decision to follow Jesus on a demanding journey for life, is very clear.

The Goal of Formation – a Relationship

What else is this call about? It is not just about what one is asked to turn away from; more positively, it is about a *relationship with Jesus,* and a life-time of learning through engagement in his mission. In practical terms it is about participation in creating and sustaining kingdom spaces and times in society and in our own communities.

It is clear that the pastoral and missionary aspects of discipleship are inextricably linked: caring for the faith community and going beyond its confines to the nations. As the disciples journey with Jesus, they witness his healings and they hear his teaching, both that which is directed to the wider public, and that which was especially given to them. Ultimately, they will see that Jesus' vision and mission, while directed initially to the 'lost sheep' of the house of Israel, has implications for the whole world – for 'the nations' – and they will respond by going to the ends of the known world. They will become engaged in encounters which would originally have been thought impossible. Today, such encounters include the believers, unbelievers, and truth-seekers who populate our world.

The Praxis Approach

Jesus shared his life and work particularly with those disciples whom the gospel writers call apostles, those very closely and immediately associated with the Kingdom of God project. We know from the gospel text itself, that there were other close disciples including (most unusually at the time) many women.

Despite the ideal learning conditions – modelling, accompaniment, the sharing of life and mission, demonstrations, and direct instruction – the gospels depict the disciples as very slow learners. Mark's is the grimmest picture of their failure at many levels, but it is simply a matter of degree in terms of the depiction in the other gospels.

Donald Senior points to the human tendency to idealise key players when accounts of their lives and works are written some years after their death. The fact that the disciples are depicted as being very slow to pick up on Jesus' values and messages, indicates that the original disciples were indeed slow to understand, so much so that even the tendency to idealisation could not lessen their limitations. One can also reasonably assume that this depiction highlights difficulties the leaders were having with certain of the disciples in the gospel writers' own communities (cf. Mk 6:51–52 and Mk 8:17–21).

Peter as Disciple

As depicted quite fully in all four gospels, Peter's journey into discipleship illustrates many of the points one can make about the disciples as a group, particularly their incapacity to grasp the essentials of the Kingdom of God. Peter failed very publicly to understand the nature of the kingship of the person whom he believed to be the Messiah. He was attracted to the idea of earthly power, and was severely reprimanded for that. Jesus refers to him as 'Satan' (Mk 8:33) and an obstacle to Jesus' mission (Matt 16:23). Extraordinarily harsh descriptors!

The disciples' deepest failure was to abandon Jesus in his time of greatest trial – his passion and death. In this regard two disciples stand out as failing more miserably than the others – Judas who betrayed him for thirty pieces of silver, and Peter who denied knowing him when confronted by a servant girl. The others simply disappeared, although Jesus' mother and John were with him at the end.

During Jesus' life, Peter had received special privileges such as witnessing the transfiguration of Jesus. He also was one of the prime witnesses of Jesus' resurrection. Subsequently, Peter is given an explicit leadership role among the disciples (Matt 16:18–19; Lk 22:31–32; Jn 21:15–19). He is the leader among a group who will each in turn go on to become important leaders in the newly emerging Church.

Jesus' formation of his disciples does not seem, on the face of it, to have been very successful, but the story does not end with the sorry episode of their desertion in time of trial. The gospel accounts of Jesus' resurrection and final days with the disciples see him persevering with his forgiveness and compassion and encouragement.

> *The disciples' record was not good. They complained, they misunderstood, they quarreled, they deserted, they denied. Only one was lost. But the part of the story that becomes 'gospel' – 'good news' – is that in the face of the master they failed, the disciples detected the infinite compassion of God, and they committed this memory to the Church.*[6]

Because of this infinite compassion, in every age members of faith communities are empowered to continue with the work of formation just as Jesus did, against the odds.

Many dioceses and systems have impressive frameworks to guide the local processes of formation. It is wise to be well acquainted with these and to access some of the other excellent material available via the internet.

A short passage from a recent framework prepared by the National Catholic Education Commission encapsulates some of the goals of this challenge:

> *The intention of formation for mission is to enable:*
>
> - *Deeper faith relations with God, self, Church, others, and creation*
>
> - *Greater engagement between individuals' lives marked by 'accompaniment' in the service of others*
>
> - *A culture of dialogue*
>
> - *Stronger commitment to the ministry of teaching and parenting*
>
> - *A deeper call into missionary discipleship.*[7]

Reflection

An important insight from the gospel is that Jesus' disciples had to learn on the job and they proved to be slow learners despite Jesus' best efforts. This must be encouraging news for all teachers. Jesus didn't get the job done in his lifetime, but he sent the Holy Spirit to finish the job, and by any definition this was accomplished in the experience of the early Christian communities. We live in a time when it is necessary to recall that the support offered by the Holy Spirit is as available to us as it was to Jesus' first disciples.

1. What experiences speak to you about God's presence in your world? In your work?

2. How good are you at reflecting on your experiences, making sense of them, and learning from them? How much time do you put into this?

The Catholic Communities of the Hampden Region

St Patrick's Day 2018 will forever be etched into the minds and hearts of the people of the Hampden region in south-western Victoria. On the evening of this day, fires swept through the farming communities of Camperdown and Terang, causing devastating loss of stock and property. Three Catholic school communities were directly impacted by these fires through loss experienced by the families of students and staff. This devastation, however, produced an opportunity for an expression of mission through life-giving pastoral ministry.

The principals and leadership teams of St Thomas's Terang and St Patrick's Primary and Mercy Regional College Camperdown met during the affected weekend and realised that they would need to be in dialogue amongst themselves and with other agencies to plan a consolidated response that would bring relief and build confidence across their communities. In terms of effective proclamation of Good News amidst this devastating experience, it was decided that the same message should be shared across the three schools in a manner that was organised, timely and considered. Feedback later received affirmed this direction as a means of bringing certainty in uncertain circumstances.

Leadership and staff witnessed over those initial weeks by gathering in each school daily to pray and check on each other. It was decided that the Lenten focus for that year should be on raising funds for their own communities in need and explicit links were made with the wider Catholic mission imperative. For these schools and their connected parish communities, *pastoral ministry became mission in practice at their very doorstep*.

CHAPTER 3
Mission and Identity – Catholic Does as Catholic Is

Go and tell John what you have seen and heard: the blind receive their sight, the lame walk, the lepers are cleansed, the deaf hear, the dead are raised, and the poor have good news brought to them. (Luke 7:22).

'Kingdom times and spaces' are hard to define in the abstract, but we recognise what they are when we encounter them.

The identity and mission of Catholic schools are much discussed at the present time. What does 'being Catholic' mean in a postmodern context? In his *Educator's Guide to Catholic Identity*, Paul Sharkey takes the view that 'Catholic is as Catholic does'. We strongly agree that a community's identity is most accurately discerned by what its members are actually committed to, no matter what the rhetoric of the community might claim in official documents like mission statements. What we commit to in terms of time, energy, priorities, relationships, and resources is the best indication of how we view our community's religious purpose or mission.

Being Catholic: Three Approaches

The relationship between mission and identity is not only an institutional issue; it is also a personal one. We need to ask ourselves: What does it feel like to be Catholic today? What do we wish it felt like to be Catholic? What are we prepared to do to get from A to B?

Schools, systems and diocesan leaders are currently considering those questions and the organisational and formational implications of the current situation. Three recent systemic approaches indicate that Catholic school authorities are serious about probing issues of identity and mission.

(i) Catholic Schools at a Crossroad

The Bishops of NSW in 2007 published a joint statement entitled *Catholic Schools at a Crossroad*. From this we can gain some insight into their thinking as they considered the changed context of Catholic education in NSW, and the policy issues this raises for Catholic school systems.

The Bishops addressed a concern that being inclusive 'waters down' the 'Catholic' nature of the schools, and took a very clear stance for inclusivity – enrolments should be as *inclusive* as local circumstances permit.

(ii) Who's Coming to School Today?

In 2009 the Catholic Education Office Brisbane commissioned the Australian Council for Educational Research (ACER) to carry out a survey of Catholic schools in a project entitled *Who's Coming to School Today?* The aim of the project was to establish a profile of the schools' population in order to be able to target responses. Responses to the data included strengthening formation, and also adopting the ECSI project (below) to further enrich data, to enable conversation and to shape missional formation.

(iii) The Enhancing Catholic School Identity (ECSI) Project

The Catholic Education Commission of Victoria, working in partnership with the Catholic University of Leuven Belgium, has for several years sponsored the *Enhancing Catholic School Identity* (ESCI) project to explore the identity of Catholic schools at the institutional level. In the course of the project the researchers developed a model of how mission and identity intersect in the setting of a Catholic school. Based on this model they also developed a number of survey instruments to determine empirically where schools stand, and so identify an agenda to enhance their Catholic identity.

The result of this project is that schools and school systems now have a variety of rich information about the faith context in which they function. Many dioceses are currently working with this project. The question for leaders is what to do with the data, and more specifically, how to use it to best effect in enhancing the Catholic identity of their school.

These initiatives reflect a wider debate within the Australian Catholic community about what 'being Catholic' means and what the normative requirements of 'being Catholic' are today. The debate has also been shaped by research in a number of Western countries which indicates that, since the 1970s, Catholics tend to ignore normative markers of identity and to self-identify as 'being Catholic' on their own terms.[8]

In his book *Catholic Identity or Identities*, social anthropologist Gerald Arbuckle points out that there are at least eleven ways in which people identify as 'being Catholic' today.[9] These lie along a continuum running from what he terms 'conservative' to what he describes as 'progressive' with the difference being judged in terms of how people understand 'the Catholic tradition' and the associated notion of 'truth'.

Those towards the 'conservative' end see both as unchanging in nature and expression. Those at the 'progressive' end see both as in need of ongoing understanding, development, and re-expression. While the terms 'conservative' and 'progressive' have become politicised, and so not necessarily helpful, Arbuckle is rightly asking us to examine the *implied understandings* about faith, culture, and the meaning of history, which we hold.

Pope Francis wisely sidesteps the dichotomy of progressive versus conservative. He advocates *a radical position*. He points out that the important issue in Christian life, personal and communal, is commitment that reflects the concerns, message and mission of Jesus. The test of effective mission is whether or not the community assists the most needy in our societies – the poor and the marginalised. When viewed from this perspective, 'being Catholic' takes on a clearer meaning. There seems little doubt that Francis' message resonates with people of goodwill across a very wide spectrum.

A Radical Approach to Being Catholic

In this Guide we want to probe the consequences of pursuing Francis' radical approach to being Catholic by exploring its correlates: 'becoming missionary disciples' and 'carrying on the mission of Jesus'. In this perspective, there are indeed normative standards that shape what being Catholic means at the individual, communal and institutional levels. Put another way, 'Catholic does what Catholic is'. Not only can who we are as Catholics be inferred from what we do, but who we are *needs to find conscious expression in what we do*.

Identity Comes Through Story

Anthropologists suggest that personal and communal identity is conferred through narratives, which are consciously constructed stories. We come to an understanding of who we are through choosing to belong to a people with a story, and by moving more deeply into, and further shaping, that story.

Catholic identity is conferred through the narratives of mission with which we identify. Schools create their own Catholic identities by telling the story of mission through their commitments. There are great numbers of these to be found across Australia. A small number feature in this Guide.

A radical approach to Catholic schooling requires that *conscious connections be made between what happens in a local Catholic school and the message and mission of Jesus*.

Jesus' message and mission recast many assumptions about what it means to be human. While Jesus entered into history at a specific time and in a specific culture, he promised that God's Spirit would guide and empower his followers across history and in all cultures. We live in that promise.

Mission is a work of the Spirit. It evolves over time and has to be reformulated as contexts change. A mission that is not first contextualised, and then re-contextualised as eras change, is a contradiction in terms.

The mission narrative of the Catholic community is that of people who grow in understanding as they journey on together in faith and experience new things. This narrative is often marked by flawed, and sometimes complacent, understandings about how God is at work in the world. However, all attempts to narrow down the scope of God's mission are interrupted (to use theologian Lieven Boeve's term)[10] by the events of history and the cultural changes that follow.

In Pope Francis' view, 'being Catholic' today calls people to take up the mission of Jesus anew. 'Catholic' understood in this radical sense is concerned with how, in our age and culture, we understand and articulate the demands of mission and the level of commitment we bring to meeting these demands. In this context Pope Francis challenges us to become a community of 'missionary disciples'.

Having sound data on the faith context in which a local school operates is clearly a benefit in this task.

Intrinsic Connection

From a theological perspective then, identity and mission are intrinsically connected. They are, as it were, two sides of the one coin. Whenever there is confusion about identity, there will also be confusion about mission, and vice versa. The most common form of this confusion occurs when the mission of a Catholic school is de-contextualised, or taken for granted.

Mission – the way in which we make the Kingdom of God present in our context – is always *concrete and specific*. Mission is de-contextualised when it is expressed in high-sounding generalities that could be applied to any school almost anywhere.

Gerard Egan, a Catholic priest and noted U.S. psychologist, tells the story of working at Central

Command in the Pentagon with a brief to resolve tensions among the members. He began his session with the generals by asking: 'What is the mission of Central Command?' 'Let's not waste time on that' said the general in charge. 'We all know the answer.'

'Humour me,' said Egan and, with that, he produced a number of filing cards and passed them around the room. 'Will you each write down what you think Central Command's mission is?' he asked.

When the group had finished writing, he collected the cards, shuffled them, and then read each one out. Of the eleven generals present, no two agreed on what the mission of Central Command was. It took very little further discussion to clarify why there was tension in the group. When mission is taken for granted, confusion soon reigns.

Mission is Concrete and Practical

Jesus' mission was about making the Kingdom of God present in history and in the cultural settings in which people live. Thus, unless it is continues to be concrete and practical, mission does not really exist.

In a school, mission involves creating 'Kingdom spaces' within school life, initiatives that stand as a witness to living the Gospel authentically. In this radical sense 'being Catholic' is an invitation open to everyone. It goes beyond institutional adherence, inviting all in the community to commit to the Kingdom of God.

'Kingdom spaces' are hard to define in the abstract, but we do recognize what they are when we encounter them in practice. They are defined by relationships and the quality of those relationships, and thus seem to exist provisionally, always open to renewal and improvement. Kingdom spaces are perhaps best described as *places, times and encounters when the Spirit of God is clearly at work empowering people to do things for each other that at one point they would not have believed to be possible.*

Kingdom spaces are the times and places where 'mission' is translated into concrete, practical action. When they appear in the life of the school, teachers, students and parents have a sense of belonging to the school community and of being captured by its mission narrative.

It is not only, as Paul Sharkey rightly suggests, that 'Catholic is as Catholic does', but also equally the case that 'Catholic does as Catholic is'.

Reflection

We gain our identity from a number of sources, including our own narrative. Many teachers in Catholic schools have a 'Catholic' chapter in their narrative and this can be a help, or a hindrance. All narratives are a compilation of what happened and what we hoped would happen. So, they are partly true and partly untrue. Equally, all narratives contain implicit assumptions that we rarely acknowledge, or even think about, but which shape the stance we take to 'things Catholic'.

1. Reflect on the 'Catholic Chapter' in your own narrative. What are the high points? What are the low points?

2. How do these shape the stance you take to 'things Catholic'?

3. If your story were told another way, how might this change your stance?

Mission as Partnership in God's Creation
St Francis Xavier, Ballarat

Care for the Earth has been a staple of the curriculum offerings at St Francis Xavier School (SFX), Ballarat for twelve years. The Mercy Sisters set the school on this trajectory when they ventured into organic farming to feed the original boarders, the Sisters, and local poorer families. A commitment to sustainable practices and biodiversity permeates the commitment of the school to 'engender a passion for learning, respect and an ability to live in harmony with God's creation'.

School practices, such as wrapper-free lunches, recycling, building with reclaimed materials, re-vegetating unique wetlands, and growing our own organic produce, exemplify the witness offered by the school community in Caring for the Earth.

A challenge faced by the school is making links in the students' minds between caring for the earth and Christian mission in practice. We respond to this challenge by ensuring Scripture and Church teachings, especially the wisdom of Pope Francis, are made explicit in learning sequences.

Dialogue partners are an important component of the school's commitment to environmental sustainability. SFX does this by networking with other ResourceSmart schools. It has recently partnered with the Stephanie Alexander Kitchen Garden Foundation as part of the students' learning journey in preparing and sharing fresh, seasonal, delicious food.

The school also seeks to strengthen this aspect of its mission by making connections with other Catholic schools in the area to offer them ongoing support and networking opportunities.

Through their witness to and proclamation of the Gospel across a range of media platforms, SFX continues to model Pope Francis' call to enter into dialogue with all people about 'care for our common home'.

CHAPTER 4
Biblical Traditions of Mission

The creation accounts in the book of Genesis contain, in their own symbolic and narrative language, profound teachings about human existence and its historical reality. They suggest that human life is grounded in three fundamental and closely intertwined relationships: with God, with our neighbour and with the earth itself. (Pope Francis, Laudato Si', #66)

At the outset of our brief exploration into the mission of Catholic schools today, we acknowledged the centrality of Jesus' teaching on the Kingdom of God. In this chapter we put the spotlight further on aspects of mission's biblical foundations.

The Bible is a veritable library of books that bear witness firstly to a people's growing understanding of God's mission in the created universe, and secondly to their own place within that mission. The experience of these ancestors in the faith has a great deal to offer faith communities today.

A Rich Tapestry of Missional Traditions

The Bible has many missional traditions. Oral and later written traditions were reshaped from time to time as new contexts prompted Israel's leaders to understand and re-express the community's understanding of the God they worshipped and their own identity.

These traditions have different emphases and, when more than one tradition encompasses a similar area of Israel's life, though different in emphasis, they often complement each other. The wise editors of the Biblical material generally dealt with such pluralism, not by attempting to integrate the various traditions, but by including both, sometimes side by side, within the text.

There is a similar situation in the New Testament. Four Gospels, each an authentic but different response by a community and its leader to Jesus' life and message, are included in their integrity within the Biblical text.

In Biblical terms, mission embraces the grand sweep of God at work within history. It extends from the beginning of creation, through the story of a particular people, and culminates in that of Jesus as God's mission incarnate. It concludes with Jesus' disciples carrying his mission of love, healing and relationship to the ends of the earth.

While at first sight it might seem that mission has little to do with the Old Testament, the Old Testament is rich in missional insights in the sense of mission described above. In fact, there are *many traditions and theologies of mission* in both the Old and New Testaments. Each is the result of *theological reflection*, undertaken by faith leaders in the circumstances in which their communities found themselves.

In our brief summary, we will touch on five of the Old Testament's important mission models. Each was significant in the religious culture which shaped Jesus and his early disciples. Each has ongoing relevance for mission within the life of the Church and its many faith-based groups.

Tradition 1. Mission as Liberation and Community Building – the Exodus Tradition[11]

The first tradition relates to the foundation story, the myth, which in fact is the deepest truth. The community of Israel established its identity around this story: the Exodus tradition. This tradition emerges from an experience of liberation from oppression. It depicts the physical and spiritual pilgrimage of a liberated people towards deeper understanding of who God was for them and, as a consequence, who they were to be in relationship to God, each other and the whole created world.

As we have noted, the accounts of God's dealings with the people of Israel include a number of separate traditions. Sometimes these traditions have different strands within them. In regard to Israel's origins as a liberated people, for example, one strand of the Exodus tradition places the emphasis on the *diversity of those origins* – the motley groups of various backgrounds who escaped from slavery in Egypt, went into the desert, and were fashioned into a people with whom God made a covenant.

A second strand emphasises the *final result* of the process – *the unity* of a people who were the product of the shared covenant experience. Both strands of the Exodus tradition contain important, complementary, elements of an overall narrative of God's mission in regard to Israel.

The Exodus tradition acknowledges that it is the life of a people, *as a people*, which is the vehicle for God's purpose. The foundational experience of Exodus is one of freedom from slavery, and then of journey in which a people gradually constructs a common identity based on a shared hope.

Central to this identity was the covenant forged between themselves and God. With it came the call to be a *contrast society*, a people who 'did life differently', who made the widows, orphans and aliens (code for the marginalised) the centre of their concern.

In his gospel many centuries later, Matthew was to touch into the centrality of the covenant relationship. In introducing Jesus, Matthew constructed a genealogy which included his descent from four women who were marginalised either by ethnic origin or by their personal situation. Such an approach was unusual within an extremely patriarchal society in which women were particularly vulnerable. By constructing his genealogy of Jesus in this way, Matthew was reminding his predominantly Jewish community that, for God, the true meaning of the covenant runs very deep. God has sent the Messiah and he has socially unacceptable elements to his heritage!

The core of the Exodus tradition of mission is that our relationships with God and our fellow humans should exist *in balance*, meaning that each is the touchstone for the authenticity of the other. In Israel's long history, whenever things became out of balance, prophets were called forth by God to demand that the balance be restored.

The themes of *journey into the unknown* and *renewal* in the Exodus tradition were to appear again and again in Israel's faith history. Through prophets and other leaders, God called the people to regroup, to recommit to a shared community life, and to recognise God's loving relationship played out in the demanding circumstances of people's lives.

The Exodus tradition provides an interpretative framework for those committed to mission in situations of gross marginalisation and alienation. Such situations exist in every society, and between societies across the globe. The Exodus tradition guides missional disciples in bearing witness to the values and experience of liberation, community, and inclusion across life's journey.

Tradition II – Mission as Journey of Faith into the Unknown – the Abraham Tradition

The Abraham tradition of mission takes a step back in time from the Exodus model. It too involves a journey theme. Abraham's journey is also a physical and a spiritual one. Like the Exodus tradition, the Abraham tradition involves seeing the world through a different lens, judging it by different values. It calls the missional disciple to the *self-emptying demanded by faith*.

Both Moses and Abraham leave behind a polytheistic culture and journey into the unknown. In Abraham's case, despite God's promise of a land and that he would be the father of many nations, his life's journey ends without it being obvious how this was to be brought about. Although through God's intervention, Abraham was ultimately able to have a son, he did not live to see himself as the 'blessing to the nations' that God had promised. His life's journey was always one of hoping against hope.

Abraham's spiritual legacy is one of unwavering faith and trust in most difficult circumstances. It is foundational to all who answer God's call to move beyond their comfort zone and go wherever the call to mission takes them, no matter how unpromising the results of their efforts may seem to be. As the father in

faith of three of the world's great religions, Abraham calls us into a broad vision of God's mission, and into a trust in God at work in our world. It reminds the disciple that mission is a long-haul business and that faith and hope are essential virtues.

Tradition III – Mission as Creation

The Creation tradition takes us back even further in time, and assumes a divine plan that embraces the whole of creation, including the whole of humanity. It describes the beginning of a grand adventure with God, which continues today:

> All that contributes to the improvement of the world, to its ennoblement, all that renders it more beautiful and just, more worthy of the image of God – the arts, technology, science, justice and peace – belongs to mission understood in the broad sense as participation in creation.[12]

In this mission tradition, Israel came to understand that God's purpose is cosmic. The creation tradition of mission is a mature reflection on God and God's purpose. *It is wider in scope than the story and witness of a particular people.*

The first eleven chapters of the book of Genesis introduce us to God as the *God of the universe, and of all peoples.* In this grand introduction, the Jewish leaders who shaped the Bible taught about the unity of all of creation, and of all peoples under God. They did so by juxtaposing two traditions. In one tradition, humans are made in the image and likeness of God (*imago Dei*) and, like God, have authority over creation. However, another complementary strand of the creation tradition emphasises that humans are taken from the earth and are, in that sense, of the earth and close to the earth. Each strand of the creation tradition contains an important truth with implications for humans' roles and responsibilities as co-creators.[13] In no way can the Genesis accounts of creation appropriately be taken as justification for the exploitation of the earth.

In proper balance, the Creation tradition of mission calls for a *responsible husbanding and developing of the earth's resources*. It also calls for a recognition *that all people, regardless of race, origin or sexuality, are children of the one God.*

Model IV – Mission as Prophetic Word and Action

The terms of the covenant between God and the people demanded that relationships within Israel should mirror the kind of relationship that God offers God's people.

These fundamentals were frequently ignored or forgotten, especially by Israel's elites. In response, God called forth great prophets drawn from different walks of life who, in no uncertain terms, drew the people's attention to their failures to uphold the covenantal relationships. They reminded the people and Israel's rulers that God expected them to give witness to a right relationship with God by putting the widow, the orphan and the alien at the centre of their consideration. Without this priority, no worship of God could be deemed sincere.

Israel's prophets never let the people forget that they themselves had once been aliens and how bad that experience had been. When they had been at their lowest, God had been their liberator. No less was demanded of them regarding others.

Later, the Gospels highlighted this tradition by noting that Jesus identified with the marginalised in his own society – those suffering and in need of healing, food, and the dignity of their humanity (especially children, women, social outcasts, and aliens). Not surprisingly, people recognised Jesus as prophet (Mk 8:27-28).

Luke's Gospel creatively builds up the picture of Jesus' total identification with the marginalised beginning with the circumstances of his birth. When speaking in the synagogue of his home town, Nazareth, Jesus identifies his mission *unequivocally* with the poor and marginalised using the words of the prophet Isaiah:

> The Spirit of the Lord is upon me, because he has anointed me to bring good news to the poor.
>
> He has sent me to proclaim release to the captives and recovery of sight to the blind, to let the oppressed go free, to proclaim the year of the Lord's favour. (Lk 4:18-19).

In living out his mission, Jesus epitomised religious living at its best, in accord with the traditions of his own people. Missionary disciples are called to do no less. *This implies a sound knowledge of and love for one's religious heritage.*

Tradition V – Mission as Re-creation and Hope

The Babylonian Exile (587-539 BCE), an exile which lasted for at least two generations, was a most traumatic experience for the Jewish people. It followed the destruction of Jerusalem and the temple, the central symbols of Israel's faith, and the deportation of all but the poorest classes to a foreign land from which they had little hope of return.

Times of crisis tend to create, or bring to the surface, deep fault-lines within a society, in this instance divisions which were already existing about the identity of the community, and about how to live their Jewish faith.

Two leaders – Ezekiel and Second Isaiah[14] – responded in different ways, in their messages of comfort and the hope of new life. Different values featured in their respective blueprints for the future.

For Ezekiel, spokesperson of one tradition, the emphasis was on liturgy, worship, and a restored priesthood. He encouraged Israel to insulate its identity and traditions against those of other nations.

Second Isaiah, echoing a complementary tradition of Deuteronomy, Hosea and Jeremiah, ignored the traditional priesthood and sought to restore the common people as a 'royal priesthood'. His vision helped people make sense of the political liberation brought by the foreigner, Cyrus of Persia. Cyrus' intervention was seen by Second Isaiah as a sign of God's salvation being extended to the Gentiles. Both prophets appeal to traditions. Both were and are considered to be great prophets. The work of both was eventually included in the canon of the Bible.

In the 500 years prior to the birth of Jesus, Ezekiel's work made the greater impact in Israel's life. However, in describing his mission in his home town Nazareth, Jesus did so by appealing to the vision of Second Isaiah (Lk 4: 16-21).

The efforts made by Israel's leaders to regroup and renew after the return from exile were impressive and this, like the situation facing Christians in the West today, required imagination and wisdom. Above all, the situation demanded of both leaders and people the capacity to live with pluralism in theological matters, respecting the insights contained in diverse stances.[15] This was not in evidence in the work of some of Israel's prominent leaders such as Ezra who, faced with a mammoth rebuilding task, opted for the narrower path to renewal.

Missionary disciples are generally wise to avoid a categorical either/or approach in dealing with complex issues such as pluralism which is a feature of both society and Church today. A faithful reading of the Bible helps the disciple to see that wisdom lies in drawing on the value of many missional insights carried within the community. With the guidance of the Holy Spirit, dialogue and discernment will help get the balance right in a particular situation.

Mission Involves Looking Outwards

The Jewish people experienced themselves as chosen by God (e.g. Deut 7:7 and Exod 6:7) in a special way. *But chosen for what?* Unless they were prepared to wrestle with this question, there was a tendency for the Old Testament communities to become inward-looking and comfortable in their special relationship with God. A similar tendency exists in many Christian faith communities today. Yet mission pushes faith communities outwards, in hope, on a journey of faith.

Some within Israel came to see that God's election of Israel *was for the sake of the nations, not for its own sake*. In this sense, Israel's election had a missional intention – to be a blessing to the nations. Israel's was an experience of calling and choice with significance and responsibilities taking Israel beyond current understandings and easy interpretations.

All four gospel writers were to return to this theme – urging the post-resurrection communities to recognise themselves as communities of missional disciples. They were to go out into the whole world spreading the good news of God's saving action in Jesus by proclaiming the good news of the Kingdom of God to the whole of creation (Mark 16:16-18; Matt 28:16-20).

When these communities witnessed to human dignity and the equality of all, particularly the marginalised, they flourished and multiplied, despite persecution. The Gospel process they initiated continued, literally, to the ends of the known world.

At its best, *the quality of Israel's communal life* raised questions in the minds of neighboring peoples about the God whom they worshipped. Israel's translation of core values into deeds becomes the hermeneutical key for successive generations. So too it was with the early disciples of Jesus, and continues with faith communities today.

In presenting the mission, deeds and teaching of Jesus of Nazareth, the New Testament writers engaged very creatively with the five missional models featured in this chapter as part of their heritage. Through their reflective and imaginative work, they in turn produced a library of scriptures which we know as the New Testament – a magnificent witness to God's mission made manifest in Jesus and in the life of the early Church.

Reflection

The Judeo-Christian tradition is not exempt from the tendency for human groupings, once established, to focus inward. Despite many experiences of God's creating, liberating and forgiving action, and the persistent calls for renewal, the tendency to self-absorption has continued. It must be resisted for the health of the community.

1. In what ways does your school look outwards to the good of the wider communities – local, national, global, and cosmic – in which it is embedded?

2. How central are such activities to the way the school understands its purpose and identity?

3. Who are the school's partners in these activities, and how does it relate to them?

Mission as Peace and Reconciliation
St Patrick's College, Ballarat

The Royal Commission into Institutional Responses to Child Sexual Abuse highlighted a group of past students from St Patrick's College Ballarat whose abuse had never been genuinely acknowledged. Through a process of deliberate and respectful dialogue with survivors, the College was able to shine a light on past abuse, name it as part of the school's history, publicly apologise for what had been done, and witness to a College community where truth is honoured.

There is a cost in witnessing to the gospel message of Jesus in this way. Seeking reconciliation and honouring truth has led to the removal of some names from school honour boards. Our experience has been that acknowledging and owning past wrongs is an uncomfortable experience for some in the extended community. *Trust is not rebuilt overnight.*

The student body sought to find its own voice in the process of reconciliation. It wrote an open letter to the community expressing its sorrow at the pain and the grief of survivors, and acknowledging that past crimes must be confronted and discussed. The letter expressed the students' confidence that the College now builds pride and dignity in its students.

The college has a willing dialogue partner in the Old Collegians network in pursuing this agenda. It provides pastoral and practical support to survivors (and other Old Boys) in need.

The school community has learned that dealing with grief, such as that created by sexual abuse, involves addressing deeply held, but rarely expressed feelings, and that this is best done symbolically. A reflective garden and monument – the first of its type in the region – was constructed at the front of the College and stands as a witness and a permanent reminder to new generations of students, teachers and their families, of those who were previously forgotten. The garden symbolises the school's ongoing commitment to a journey towards renewing trust, engendering hope, and expressing commitment to ongoing vigilance in matters of young people's safety.

CHAPTER 5
Catholic Schools – Mission Within a Worldwide Family

Do not be disheartened in the face of the difficulties that the educational challenge presents! Educating is not a profession but an attitude, a way of being; in order to educate it is necessary to step out of ourselves and be among young people, to accompany them … Give them hope and optimism for their journey in the world. Teach them to see the beauty and goodness of creation and of man who always retains the Creator's hallmark. But above all with your life be witnesses of what you communicate. (Pope Francis)[16]

Many factors interact in shaping the Church's understanding of its mission in Catholic education today. In the 1980s and 1990s, for example, when congregational leaders and leaders of Catholic Education Offices in Australia first sought to assist Catholic schools to articulate their mission, they did so out of a conviction that *mission is local before it is anything else*.

At the same time, there was an emerging recognition of the necessary role of leadership across the community of schools. Systems were developed to handle the funding, as per Government requirement, but also to provide leadership in the increasingly complex environments in which schools were operating.

In the spirit of communion within the broader Church community, system leaders now partner local school communities in terms of vision, processes and opportunities that cannot be provided locally, at least not to the same or to a sufficient, degree.

Beyond this stands a further level of support. Leadership from the popes and from the Vatican agency responsible for Catholic education (the Congregation for Catholic Education) provides a strong framework of values and understandings within which all Catholic schools construct their mission and identity.

A Worldwide Family

In recent decades, significant leadership has come from these sources. Because it is addressed to communities across the world, pastoral guidance from the centre is generally expressed in broad terms. In consequence, local leaders must make sense of it in their own contexts.

Prior to the Second Vatican Council (1962-5) papal guidance on Catholic schooling in the form of official documents had been infrequent[17], and very much tied to societal and cultural agendas that are no longer applicable.

The lack of documented guidance prior to Vatican II also reflected the assumption that the religious congregations, operating within the framework of the great spiritual traditions of education, provided the necessary leadership in the schools for which they were responsible.

Guidance from Vatican II

Aware that official teaching was lagging behind developments on the ground, and that there were new issues requiring attention, those managing the Council established a commission to place Catholic schooling on the official agenda. The commission drew up a working document.

The assembled bishops rejected the document because its scope was deemed to be too narrow; it did not, for example, address issues as experienced in developing countries. Bishops from outside Europe were dealing with pastoral situations in which young people's basic right to education often went unacknowledged. They wanted a statement from

the Council committing the Church to work for recognition of this basic human right.

Marrying this agenda substantively to that of Catholic schooling as experienced in other countries proved difficult. Between 1963 and 1965 the commission produced five drafts in an attempt to build a consensus. With the Council drawing to a close, a statement of twelve agreed principles that should shape the Church's involvement in education was finally agreed upon. This document, *The Declaration on Christian Education (Gravissimum Educationis), was accepted*. The understanding was that there would be further attention given to Catholic schooling in the years after Vatican II.

The Catholic School 1977

Taking up the challenge, in 1977 the Congregation for Catholic Education issued *The Catholic School*, which remains a seminal statement on Catholic schooling even today.

The Catholic School established four basic positions crucial to the mission of a Catholic school. The Catholic school:

- endeavours to help students develop a worldview in which life, culture and faith, are integrated

- aims to provide all its members with the experience of being part of a faith community

- seeks to create a milieu in which it is possible to nurture virtues central to a Christian character.

- aspires to reach the same standards of excellence in curriculum and pedagogy as other forms of schooling

Of course, each of these principles has to be interpreted in context. The contexts continue to change and indeed have done so radically since 1977.

In the early post-Vatican II period, the understanding of mission developed at the Council had little impact on the Vatican documents on Catholic schooling. For example, in 1975 Pope Paul VI issued his *Evangelii Nuntiandi (The Evangelisation of Peoples)*, summarising the insights of the 1974 synod on evangelisation – a document regarded as a magna carta of mission and evangelisation. However, it made little or no obvious impact on the development of *The Catholic School*.

Reading *The Catholic School* one can legitimately wonder why the two areas of Church life – mission and education – were developing along parallel lines. The same could be said of other areas like liturgy, social justice engagement, and areas of study such as biblical studies.

By the early 2000s, mission was beginning to be understood as the integrating idea for all of Church life, its very reason for existence, but that deep learning is taking some time to be grasped. The Catholic community struggles with this even today.

In Australia, the reception of *The Catholic School* and other subsequent documents spoke to a Catholic experience that was very different from that of many other countries. The documents reflected, for example, a perspective in which religious, rather than lay Catholic educators were predominantly responsible for Catholic schooling. The situation emerging rapidly in Australia at the time was very different.

Key Documents

The Congregation for Catholic Education has now produced a number of documents that expand on themes laid down in *The Catholic School* as well as those thrown up by new missional environments. The following is a list, with important themes, of the most influential post-Vatican II documents on Catholic education:

The Catholic School (1977)

- Community nature of Catholic schools
- Core project – integrating life with faith and culture with faith

Lay Catholics in School: Witnesses to Faith (1982)

- Lay vocation is not about plugging gaps when there are not enough religious
- Lay people have a unique vocation and competence to bring the Gospel to the world.
- In schools this involves the integration of life, culture and faith in the learning areas and includes, but goes beyond, Religious Education as a specific course of study.

The Religious Dimension of Education in a Catholic School (1988)

- Takes up the discussion on the religious dimension of Catholic schools under the following headings:
  - the educational climate
  - the personal development of each student
  - the relationship established between culture and the Gospel
  - the illumination of all knowledge with the light of faith

The Catholic School on the Threshold of the Third Millennium (1997)

- Addressed to the new context – the crisis of values, pluralism, marginalisation of the Christian faith
- Calls for a new missional commitment
- References the marginalised and the poor in particular

Consecrated Persons and their Mission in Schools: Reflections and Guidelines (2002)

- Call to religious to value their prophetic presence in schools
- Role in formation of students
- Importance of relationships
- Complements *Lay Catholics in Schools* issued twenty years earlier

Educating Together in Catholic Schools: A Shared Mission between Consecrated Persons and the Lay Faithful (2007)

- The communion between educators, religious and lay, is emphasised as essential for missional witness
- Importance of formation of staff

Educating to Intercultural Dialogue (2013)

- Education for intercultural dialogue – a central goal of Catholic education
- Treatment of culture clearer and more adequate than in previous documents
- Practicalities of dialogue in Catholic schools included

The lag between official statements and present realities has meant that leaders in Australian Catholic schools have operated on *the frontiers of possibility* in global Catholic education. The result has been that school leaders have often developed an independence of thought and a breadth of imagination some Church leaders find disconcerting. However, this has been a particular strength of Australian Catholic education and a source of its vitality.

Australian educators continue to open up a range of experiences that often lie beyond the imaginal horizon of their colleagues in other places. Many have undertaken theological studies and have been able to forge links between developing reflections on Catholic schooling and the place of the Catholic school within expanding conceptions of mission.

Mission and Identity Revisited

The Church has responsibility to carry on the mission of Jesus. How this responsibility is formulated becomes critical in understanding what it means to be Catholic. When historical consciousness shifts and people envisage a new social order, change occurs, for better or worse, and the Church's understanding of its mission generally expands in response. Shifts in historical consciousness re-define what it means to be human in important ways. This results in cultural change.

Cultural change often marginalises groups of people and so creates new mission demands. It also opens up new possibilities. At the present time refugees are a case in point. What we understand as 'Kingdom spaces' today differs in important ways from the ways we might have envisaged them as recently as the 1990s or the 2000s.

Developments in Mission Thinking

Changes in the Church's mission thinking grow out of the efforts *made to address needs in particular contexts*. Over time, they take on universal significance. The Church's mission thinking expands as its mission practice expands. The Australian experience makes an important contribution to this widely shared self-understanding.

Catholic schools are caught up in this development because they operate *at the interface between the Church and people in need*. This projects them beyond the four vital but rather inward-looking principles outlined above (*The Catholic School 1977*) into the wider world of mission.

Just as the official reflection on Catholic schooling has expanded in response to a changing educational context, so too has the Church's understanding and expression of what carrying forward Jesus' mission means within the context in which it must occur.

Because mission can take many forms, the invitation is there for all to engage in mission depending on the gifts or capacities they bring.

The Whole Community in Mission

All members of a school community can, and usually do, make a contribution to the overall mission of the school. In this sense 'mission' is an inclusive concept, an invitation to engage with and become part of the local mission narrative with genuine links, via the long Catholic narrative, to Jesus and his mission.

A singular focus on 'identity' separated from mission often carries with it fundamentalist and exclusivist overtones that fail to invite, include, or engage.

Mission and identity have to be seen together. Separating them is counterproductive and counter-intuitive. Sound mission equates to strong identity.

Reflection

This chapter sets out the four foundational mission directions for the Catholic school (see *The Catholic School*, 1977). These continue to be of major importance to Catholic schooling.

1. Using a scale of one to seven, rate each according to the importance given to it in your school.

2. Sum up the ratings from the group and determine the overall order.

3. How do you interpret the results?

4. What does this say about the school's priorities in pursuing its mission?

5. These priorities were first set out in 1977. How would you reword/rework them for 2020? What effect would this have on their order of importance?

Mission as Inter-religious Dialogue of Life
St Mary's, Swan Hill

St Mary's Primary School Swan Hill is situated in a multi-cultural and interreligious community on the Murray River in Victoria. The school's population is a blend of Catholic families from a range of ethnic communities, as well as many students coming from families of other faiths, including Sikh, Buddhist, Muslim and Hindu. The school presently has a number of Vietnamese and Afghani migrant and refugee families. As well, St Mary's maintains its traditional strong links with the Italian community. Mission in practice for this Catholic primary school is informed by, and responds to, this diversity.

St Mary's is a welcoming community driven by a commitment to maximise the educational outcomes of all students irrespective of their cultural backgrounds. Faithful to their Josephite heritage, Mary MacKillop's advice of *'never seeing a need without doing something about it'* finds expression, as a genuine witness to the Good News of Jesus, in the employment of a range of learning support officers proficient in cultural linguistic skills such as Mandarin and Vietnamese. Special attention is given to Sikh vegetarian requirements during any community gathering, and provision is made for the regulations governing Muslim students fasting during Ramadan month.

The school's mission to affirm and celebrate diversity was proclaimed recently during Harmony Day celebrations where, as part of an arts project, large murals were created capturing students with face-painted flags representing the array of nations within the school. Flags were placed around the school's gymnasium, which is also used by the wider community.

Community partnerships are an important element in recognising diversity and promoting dialogue. Staff, students and families are actively involved in the Swan Hill Cultural Diversity Week where in 2017 they participated in the HOME Swan Hill project, which saw 1200 tiny wooden homes constructed based on the question: *What does home mean to you?* Students constructed their own miniature habitats that reflected the cultural particularity that defined their sense of home. These were included in an art installation at the Swan Hill Regional Art Gallery.

Interreligious dialogue is continually present in the life and mission practice of St Mary's community, as we respond to the diversity and cultural makeup of families in our school.

CHAPTER 6
Mapping Mission Across Time

… for the Church it is a question not only of preaching the Gospel in ever wider geographic areas or to ever greater numbers of people, but also of affecting and as it were upsetting, through the power of the Gospel, mankind's criteria of judgment, determining values, points of interest, lines of thought, sources of inspiration and models of life, which are in contrast with the Word of God and the plan of salvation. (Pope Paul VI Evangelii Nundiandi #18)

These words are taken from a much-quoted passage of Pope Paul VI in his great synthesis of the proceedings of the 1974 synod on evangelisation. They also provide a summary of mission's goals in every time and place so that people may have an opportunity to receive the Gospel, and that human cultures may be challenged, and continually improved.

The earliest members of Jesus' movement formed their identity around:

- proclaiming the Good News of what God had done in Jesus through word and deed
- celebrating Jesus' memory in the breaking of the bread
- following 'the way' that he had modelled in his lifetime.

The interplay of these elements has shaped the unfolding panorama of mission across two thousand years.

The Power of Witness in Local Contexts

In attempting to treat others as Jesus had done, his early followers set an example that attracted people to the Christian communities. It did not take long for people to see, despite some obvious failures, the caring and egalitarian way in which these functioned. These elements of Christian living were very attractive. They were what we are calling here *mission as witness*.

The missionary paradigm emerging in the New Testament can be represented schematically. We will develop this schema as new forms of mission emerge and are adopted officially in the Church. When Paul moved from one place to another to spread the Good News of Jesus and establish communities of disciples, he did so as the representative of the community he had just left; the new community, therefore, had links

	MODES OF MISSION	
	Proclamation	
Forms of Mission	by Word	by Witness
Pastoral Ministry		

Mission in Early New Testament Times

back to its sponsor. Paul was also careful to work under the authority of Peter and the Christian movement's leaders in Jerusalem.

The networking of communities enabled Paul and his successors to think and speak not only in terms of individual local groups, but of and for all these groups taken together. With this development, the Church as we know it was born. Paul used the term 'body' (e.g. 1 Cor 10:17 and Romans 12:5) to describe this early network, giving a sense of corporate identity as the 'body of Christ'. Different members built that identity using their own gifts and talents.

Very early on then, Christians became aware that not every member of a faith community serves the same function, nor are all communities the same. Carrying on Jesus' mission has to be thought through in local contexts, but also in terms of the whole Church and the gifts given by the Holy Spirit to empower people into mission.

We know a great deal about Paul the great missionary because he figures so prominently in the New Testament but in the very early centuries, the good news of Jesus was spread predominantly by ordinary Christians. They could not and did not work the way Paul was called to do. They were people of all sorts, both those whose business took them around the known world of the time, and those who never left local neighbourhoods. Bevans and Shroeder, in their encyclopaedic treatment of mission theology and practice, present a picture of local folks gossiping the Gospel as they went about their daily lives. The early Christians

> ... went everywhere spreading the good news that had brought joy, release, and a new life to themselves. This must often have been not formal preaching, but the informal chattering of friends and chance acquaintances, in homes and wine shops, on walks, and among market stalls. They went everywhere gossiping the gospel; they did it naturally, enthusiastically, and with the conviction of those who are not paid to say that sort of thing. Consequently, they were taken seriously, and the movement spread, notably among the lower classes.[18]

This process of mission, in the midst of everyday life, contains elements essential for us today – the sharing of good news as we live, work and develop relationships, a form of mission authenticated by generous Christian living.

Post-Pauline Paradigm

By the time the Gospel of Matthew was written, around 80 AD, a generation or so after Paul, the ritual life of the Church was being codified, as were its leadership structures. Leaders had to make arrangements both for communal worship and for the pastoral tasks of caring for the community. The understanding of Christian life and its missional context was expanding.

As we have seen, proclamation by both witness and word emerged early as essential *modes of mission.* However, the kind of care that community members needed had to be discerned, and to assume appropriate forms such as the distribution of food, care for widows, pooling and sharing of resources, dealing with those who wanted to join the community, managing conflict, and maintaining the quality of Christian life. Sound and effective teaching continued to be a priority. As in Old Testament times, so in the first

	MODES OF MISSION	
	Proclamation	
Forms of Mission	by Word	by Witness
Pastoral Ministry		
Prayer and Liturgy		

Mission in Post-Apostolic Times

Christian communities, the authenticity of communal worship continued to be tested by the pastoral care of the community, especially service to the most vulnerable. So the mission paradigm expanded. By the end of the first century AD, the expectation that Jesus would soon return, as Paul anticipated, was beginning to fade. Those associated with pastoral responsibilities found they had to think and plan in a wider and longer-term framework than had their predecessors. Christian communities not only had to be supported in following the way of Jesus, but they had to know and be able to articulate why they were doing so in times and places very different from those of Jesus' life and ministry So, the paradigm of mission and mission theology, developed further.

During the first three centuries, the Christian communities suffered persecution from the Jews and the Romans. When, in the fourth century, the emperor Constantine, and his successor Theodosius I, made Christianity part of the state apparatus of the Roman empire, the leadership structures and rituals of faith were given a legal force that was initially very welcome. However, the state-sanctioned approval tended to breed complacency, and with it a diminution of missional zeal.

The Monastic Model of Mission

As the Roman Empire descended into chaos and broke up, the Christian monastic movement that had begun as an individual, and later as a communal, way of life in the desert, moved into the heartland of Rome's Western and Eastern empires.

Monks carried the gospel to the peripheries of the known world, for example, to the countries we know today as Ireland and the U.K. From there, it would eventually flow back into Europe and be adopted by tribes that had swept into the weakened Roman empire with destructive force.

The great missionary movement from Ireland into Europe in the sixth century, under the leadership of the Irish monk Columban (543-615), took hold of the popular imagination, and proved a most effective model of mission. The Church in the West reclaimed its evangelical fervour. Similar missionary movements were to occur in areas we now know as Eastern Europe.

The mission developed further in the medieval period with the foundation of new groups such as the Franciscans (Francis of Assisi c 1181–1226) and Dominicans (Dominic Guzman 1170–1221). The members of these groups were not bound to the model of monastic life. They were thus more flexible in bringing the Gospel to those who had not heard it, and to those in whom its message was making little impact.

Later, Ignatius of Loyola (1491-1556), founder of the Jesuits, also developed his order in such a way as to allow for maximum flexibility in spreading the Gospel in Europe and in what was then known as the 'New World' (the Americas), and the areas of east and south Asia.

Mission Enters the Language of Faith

At this time the word 'mission', so familiar to us, had only a secular usage. In the fifteenth century, Portuguese navigators were sent down the west coast of Africa to establish bases called 'missions'. These stations were to service ships bringing gold from Africa safely to Lisbon,

	MODES OF MISSION	
	Proclamation	
Forms of Mission	by Word	by Witness
Pastoral Ministry		
Prayer and Liturgy		
Defence of Human Rights		

Mission in Age of Discovery

rather than via the risky land routes. Later, Ignatius of Loyola co-opted this secular word 'mission' to describe communities established in South America and Asia, as bases from which the Gospel could be proclaimed and further Christian communities established among the indigenous peoples.

Many of the missionaries working in the New World found themselves caught up in struggles to prevent Spanish and Portuguese colonists exploiting indigenous peoples, a theme explored in the well-known film *The Mission*. As members of religious groups took up the cause of indigenous peoples with colonial administrations, the paradigm of mission expanded again with the addition of a new form – *defence of human rights*. The pope of the time, Pope Paul III, was called on to arbitrate on the issues of human rights and justice for the now-marginalised peoples from the New World – a world hardly new to those who already lived there! The Pope ruled in support of the full human dignity of the indigenous peoples. The basis for the defence of human rights and its consideration as a key aspect of mission were laid down. This remains a most important form of mission today.

During the second expansion of Europe into Africa, Southeast Asia and Oceania in the eighteenth and nineteenth centuries, two developments – one in anthropology and the second in theology – began to shape thinking about mission among Christian churches.

(i) Insights into Culture

The first, occurring in the late 19th century, was the development of the discipline of anthropology. With this came the emergence of what is known as the *empirical concept of culture* – the idea of every people having a unique culture that could be studied. This notion of culture took some time to make an impact. Even up until the 1940s and beyond, when most people thought about culture, they did so only in terms of 'civilisation'.

In this frame of reference, European civilisation was thought to represent the high point in cultural development. Operating within this perspective, many missionaries saw their task as 'civilising' the people to whom they were sent, as well as bringing the Gospel to them. Such an attitude led to the destruction of elements of local cultures. At the same time, talented missionaries helped to preserve cultures by engaging in the vital work of recording in written form languages that were in danger of being lost, and with them the people's cultures.

For their part, anthropologists challenged the view that European cultures were somehow superior to all other cultures. They saw culture as the possession of a people that creates a more or less successful plan for living together, thus enabling people to survive in a particular physical environment.[19] Looked at from this perspective, European cultures were no more or less valuable than any others. (Of course, the same critique applied to other cultures whose members considered themselves superior such as Chinese and Japanese imperial cultures.)

The empirical view of culture also raised the question whether the version of Christian faith being presented, with its forms of liturgy and its dominant theologies, all developed in Europe, was in fact ethnocentric.

Understanding and expressing faith requires that we employ the resources of our culture (concepts, language and symbols). Authentic mission was seen to demand the deep *inculturation* of faith – that is, an understanding and expression of faith that makes sense within a people's culture.

Understood in this way, mission is particularly demanding and requires assiduous study and careful preparation of personnel. Missionary congregations varied in how well this was done. In some cases, the preparation was exemplary; in others it was non-existent. During the modern period the understanding of mission had expanded again.

(ii) Theological Insights – Missio Dei

A second major development occurred in the late 20th century, and was theological. It drew on an insight of Protestant theologian Karl Barth (1886-1968). Barth was concerned that church people were seeing mission as, first and foremost something the Church did. The Church was, they believed, the principal agent of mission. In their zeal to spread the gospel, some were being carried away by their own importance.

Barth challenged the view that mission was foundationally 'what the Church did'. His argument was that mission is in fact 'what God does'. Building on this insight, the German missiologist, Karl Hartenstein (1894-1952) coined the phrase *Missio Dei* – God's mission – reminding Christians that *God is the origin of mission* and is the first missioner. This development led to the rediscovery of the truth of which both Old and New Testament writers were very aware, but which had become submerged.

Forms of Mission	MODES OF MISSION	
	Proclamation	
	by Word	by Witness
Pastoral Ministry		
Prayer and Liturgy		
Defence of Human Rights		
Inculturation		

Mission in Colonial Era

The work of Barth, Hartenstein and others was to prove influential across the Christian churches, and helped shape the position taken by the Catholic Church in the Second Vatican Council (1962-5) – see Chapter 7.

New Forms of Mission

In the last century, and particularly in recent decades, Christians have responded generously to human brokenness and need, and the deplorable state of many of the earth's ecosystems through work for justice peace and reconciliation, human development, inter-religious dialogue, and care for the earth. Popes and episcopal conferences have written extensively on these as genuine and vital expressions of the gospel demanded by various contexts. At the same time, realisation has grown that many areas of human need are complex, and are only effectively responded to with dialogue partners.

Dialogue Emerges as a Fundamental Mode of Mission

In recent decades, growing insights into how knowledge is constructed and commitment generated have brought dialogue into sharp focus as an essential

Contemporary Mission Map

Forms of Mission	MODES OF MISSION		
	Proclamation		
	by Word	by Witness	through Dialogue
Pastoral Ministry			
Prayer and Liturgy			
Defence of Human Rights			
Inculturation			
Liberation			
Justice and Peace			
Reconciliation			
Human Development			
Inter-religious Dialogue			
Care for the Earth			
Other			

Mission in the Postmodern Era

element of effective Christian mission. Furthermore, the complexities of mission require that Christians form *dialogue partners* at many levels both within and beyond the faith community if they are to be effective in creating kingdom spaces. So important is dialogue, that we have devoted a separate chapter to it (Chapter 8).

The map above summarises much of our contemporary understanding of the scope and scale of the Church community's mission. As new needs arise, the model expands. All of the forms of mission identified above are named and discussed in the Church's official documentation.

In his fifth chapter of *Redemptoris Missio* ('The Paths of Mission') Pope John Paul II reminds Church members that

> Mission is a single but complex reality, and it develops in a variety of ways. Among these ways some have particular importance in the present situation of the Church and the world (#41).

We have already seen how proclamation and witness have been closely related since the inception of Christianity. The witness required today includes, among other things, the struggle for justice, peace and reconciliation, and care for the earth. It also requires serious attention to the culture of the society in which Christians live. Without efforts to inculturate the Gospel in one's environment, it is meaningless to those to whom it is addressed – a powerful factor to be considered by all who teach and preach the Gospel. [20]

It is enlightening to consider Catholic education in terms of each of the forms of mission that have been identified. A few moments of reflection soon reveals just how much potential Catholic education, and the teachers who work in schools, have to contribute to each of the forms of mission set out in the model above. An exercise related to the work of this chapter is to be found at the end of Chapter Nine.

Reflection

Most Catholics understand that being authentic means staying on message and walking the talk. In this chapter we make the point that mission has many forms and that mission always occurs in concrete circumstances, and addresses the needs created by those circumstances. Many school mission statements are not sufficiently concrete and so provide insufficient guidance as to the practicalities of the school's mission.

1. What forms does mission take in your school?

2. What circumstances create the needs to which this mission responds?

3. Does the rhetoric of the school's mission statement match the forms mission takes in your school?

4. If there is a discrepancy, how should it be handled?

Mission as Liberation and Freedom
St Patrick's School, Port Fairy

St Patrick's School, Port Fairy, responds to Jesus' mission to bring life in its fullness (John 10:10).

Mission as liberation and freedom for each and every student finds expression through the school's journey as a Professional Learning Community (PLC). This initiative recognises that student performance is enhanced through collaborative planning and teaching processes, where teachers and students clearly know what needs to be learnt and what success could look like for each student at the end of a learning cycle.

Focusing on Maths and Reading, teachers found the freedom to identify essential learnings that matched the needs of their students within an often crowded curriculum.

Students take ownership of their own learning through authentic dialogue opportunities between students and teacher; students with other students; and teachers collaborating with other teachers. Parents and guardians are brought into the conversation and become active partners through data pictures at the beginning and end of each learning cycle, which highlight the growth in learning of their child.

The focus on learning bears witness to the school's Mission Statement which calls on the whole school community to 'inspire and challenge each other through excellent teaching, leading to high levels of learning and achievement for all'.

Students find the PLC approach liberating as they advocate for their own learning, identifying what they need to learn at any given point. For teachers, liberation is experienced through a mindset shift which takes them from 'my students' to 'our students' shaped by collaborative planning and teaching opportunities.

Student learning development is proclaimed at the end of a term when each year level's data picture is shared with the whole school and students' growth is recognised and celebrated.

An explicit learning focus at St Patrick's encourages liberation and development through a commitment to bring fullness of life for all. In this way, we live and express our Christian mission in concrete daily practice.

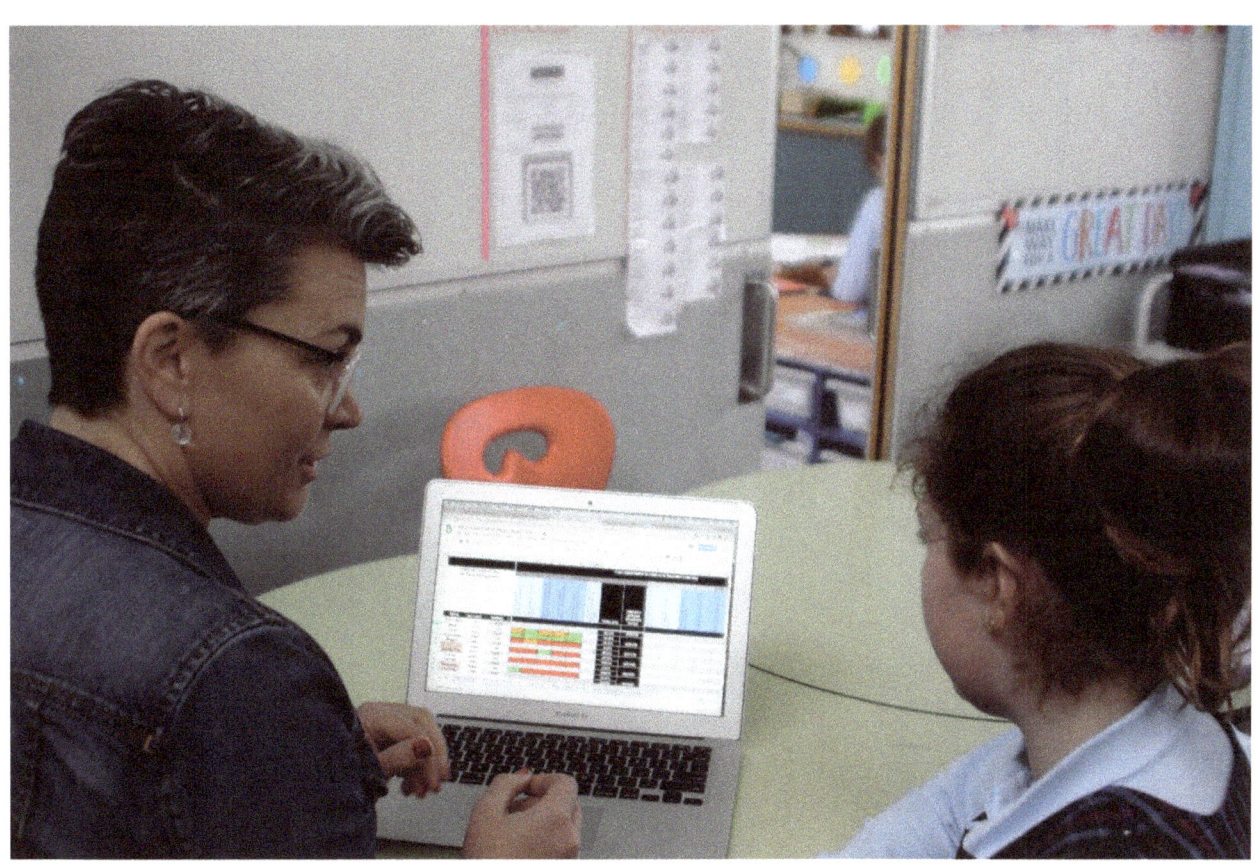

CHAPTER 7
Mission Between Peoples – An Unfolding Tradition

The Second Vatican Council (1962-65) created the platform from which further developments in Catholic mission theology have been launched. In this chapter, we trace key elements of the Catholic journey from the Council to the present.

Four key 'moments' provide a kind of navigational guide through this recent journey. These are listed below. They constitute a summary of the official guidance provided in the recent Catholic journey into mission. The journey itself continues to be played out locally in families, schools and neighbourhoods, in board rooms and businesses, and wherever humans engage in living, across the globe.

First Moment – Vatican II (1962-5)

Later in this chapter, we will note aspects of the significance of this great mission Council. Key documents with obvious missional relevance include:

- *Lumen Gentium* (*Dogmatic Constitution on the Church*)
- *Gaudium et Spes* (*Pastoral Constitution on the Church in the Modern World*)
- *Ad Gentes* (*Decree on the Church's Missionary Activity*)
- *Nostra Aetate* (*Decree on the Church's Relationship with non-Christian Religions*).

Other related documents include:

- *Dei Verbum* (*The Dogmatic Constitution on Divine Revelation*)
- *Dignitatis Humanae* (*The Degree on Religious Freedom*).

The advances in Biblical scholarship to which *Dei Verbum* gave impetus, have greatly assisted Christian communities to understand mission more deeply.

Second Moment (1975)

The synod on evangelisation was a key moment when the worldwide church leadership paused to consider progress in mission in the decade since the close of the Council.

Evangelii Nuntiandi (*On the Evangelisation of Peoples*) (EN 1975), Pope Paul VI's reflection on the synod on evangelisation of the previous year recognises that mission has *many forms*. There are, and must be, many expressions of the Kingdom of God in society and culture if faith communities are to be responsive to need. EN is sometimes called the 'magna carta' of mission theology and practice.

Third Moment (1990)

Redemptoris Missio (*On the Permanent Validity of the Church's Missionary Mandate, 1990*) (RM), encyclical of Pope John Paul II. This letter provides a comprehensive discussion of mission. It devotes a chapter (Chapter 2) to the Kingdom of God, and introduces a much-quoted discussion on the importance of dialogue. Associated with this is another key document, *Dialogue and Proclamation* (1991) from the Pontifical Council for Inter-religious Dialogue.

Fourth Moment

Key missional documents of this period to date are from Pope Francis:

Evangelii Gaudium (*The Joy of the Gospel*, 2013)
Laudato Si' (*Care for our Common Home*, 2015)
Gaudete et Exsultate (*Rejoice and be Glad*, 2018)

Important Themes

First Moment – The two great documents of Vatican II that deal with the Church – *Lumen Gentium* (LG) and *Gaudium et Spes* (GS) – are, each in different ways, profoundly missional in character. They demonstrate clearly that identity and mission are, and should be seen to be, intimately linked in the case of the Church.

Lumen Gentium sets a direction, which has continued to frame mission theology, by utilising the graphic kingdom images from the synoptic gospels in its description of the Church such as seed, little flock, salt, light. (*LG* #5). The Church is at the service of the Kingdom of God.

Gaudium et Spes addresses the Church's relationship with the modern world by identifying the Church as in solidarity with humanity, both in its joys and sorrows (#1). Although designated a 'pastoral' constitution, *GS* is in its entirety, also a missional document as is clear from its subject matter. Its theological methodology, a discernment of the 'signs of the times', continues to underpin mission theology today.

Gaudium et Spes also addresses the theme of the relationship between faith and culture, which remains a key challenge in mission. This relationship is central to the meaning-making processes in which educators engage when they work in Catholic education.

Perhaps ironically, the insight from Vatican II that summarised most succinctly the new paradigm of mission, is to be found in the document dealing with what were called in the past the 'foreign missions' (*Ad Gentes*):

> The pilgrim Church is missionary by her very nature, since it is from the mission of the Son and of the Holy Spirit that she draws her origin in accordance with the decree of God the Father...
>
> This decree flows from the fount-like love... of God the Father... (*AG* 2)

The final point in the quotation is vital in understanding the magnitude of the paradigm shift being expressed here. Mission's nature and source comes from the very life of God, a life of over-flowing love. *Mission is firstly what God does.*

The Council Fathers drew the attention of the whole Church to the fact that, since mission is first and foremost God's work, Church communities and individuals are privileged participants in what God is effecting in the world. *This understanding provides the basis for the Church's dialogue with the world.*

Jesus is the exemplar for how God's mission is to be effected in time. His mission becomes the human and very concrete expression of the disciples' mission. The Kingdom of God is the goal of Jesus' mission, as it is of the mission of the Church. The Church's role is to be at the service of the world and its people so that they may reach their destiny in God. During the decades following Vatican II, faith communities across the globe would wrestle with the implications of the paradigm shift in mission understanding.

In *Nostra Aetate* (*Declaration on the Relation of the Church to Non-Christian Religions*) (NA) the bishops provided a perspective on a new and broader understanding of salvation. This perspective recognises that God has been at work in the world since the beginning of time among all peoples and cultures. In this, the shortest of the Council's documents, the Church is specifically called upon to collaborate with members of other religions 'to preserve and encourage the moral truths' found among their adherents (*NA* #2).

There is an implicit acknowledgement in this document that faithful adherents of other religions attain salvation through their religious traditions. At the same time there is also a reaffirmation of the duty that Christians have to witness to their own faith.

Two truths of faith are finely balanced here – God's universal and effective will that all be saved, and the unique role of Jesus as universal saviour. Exploration of these issues continues, and is likely to be the subject of theological work well into the future.

Second Moment

Evangelii Nuntiandi (EN) is Pope Paul VI's reflection on the synod on evangelisation. It reaffirmed the central missional insight referred to above, that mission is a sharing in the life of God, and acknowledged the insights of *Nostra Aetate*. It clarified key elements in the emerging field of mission studies by:

- reclaiming the theology of the Kingdom of God as a basis for mission

- identifying conversion as vital for the evangelising church itself, as well as those to whom the good news is offered

- recognising that evangelisation applies not only to persons, but also to human institutions and cultures
- presenting evangelising mission as multi-faceted – for example, justice as integral to mission
- identifying the central place of proclamation through word and witness
- accepting that the unique way local peoples express their faith, 'popular religiosity', is to be not only respected, but also valued.

Evangelii Nuntiandi continues to be regarded as a seminal document.

Evangelii Nuntiandi also emphasised the need for Christians to speak to the hope that is in them on the grounds that witness must be articulated if it is to be effective.

> Always be ready to given an explanation to anyone who asks you for a reason for your hope (1 Peter 3:15).

Because it was not a major theme of the synod, dialogue does not make an appearance in *Evangelii Nuntiandi* despite Paul VI's earlier treatment of it in his first encyclical *Ecclesiam Suam (On the Church,* 1964).

> *The Kingdom of God is not a concept, a doctrine, or a program subject to free interpretation, but it is before all else a person with the face and name of Jesus of Nazareth, the image of the invisible God.*
>
> *(RM #18)*

Third Moment

Pope John Paul II's *Redemptoris Missio (Mission of the Redeemer)* (RM) was promulgated in 1990 as the change in human consciousness known as post-modernity gathered pace, and in the context of a new phase of globalisation.

There was an influential school of thought at the time which held that the era of mission 'ad gentes' was over, on the grounds that Christian communities had been established in almost all countries of the world. Pope John Paul II challenged this view.

Important elements of *Redemptoris Missio* include:

- A reminder of the need to persevere in proclaiming the Gospel.
- An affirmation, in terms of an entire chapter (ch 2), of the centrality of the Kingdom of God
- A correction that the Kingdom of God is not an ideology and must not be equated solely with achievements in the here and now
- An admonition that the Kingdom of God should not be equated entirely with earthly projects
- A further admonition that understanding of the Kingdom of God should not be separated from Christ or his Church
- An affirmation that Jesus is the Kingdom of God incarnate
- An emphasis on the key importance of dialogue in response to globalisation and the religious pluralisation of societies
- A call for a 'new evangelisation' (RM#3)

In a beautiful and much-quoted passage, the Pope reminded Catholics that Jesus is the perfect manifestation of the Kingdom:

> The Kingdom of God is not a concept, a doctrine, or a program subject to free interpretation, but it is before all else a person with the face and name of Jesus of Nazareth, the image of the invisible God. (RM #18)

As understood by Pope John Paul II, dialogue can take place at a number of levels (*RM* #57). *Dialogue of life* sees people living together as friends; *dialogue of action* enables people to come together around a common project such as work for justice and peace, or the education of young people; *dialogue of religious experience*, or what might be termed a dialogue of spiritualities, enables people to understand each other's experience in being people of faith, and in some cases this enables them to pray together; *dialogue of theological exchange* proceeds, both formally and informally, between those with theological expertise.

Under the impact of the changing nature of Australian society, and with the guidance of Pope John Paul II's work, many initiatives in inter-faith dialogue have developed.

Redemptoris Missio's call for a 'new evangelization' (*RM* #3), specifically named three groups to whom the Gospel should be directed: those who have never heard the Gospel; those in whom the light of faith has grown dim; and the community of the faithful (*RM* ##31-32).

Fourth Moment

This new moment was officially ushered in by Pope Francis' reflection on the work of 2012 synod on the new evangelisation – *Evangelii Gaudium* (*The Joy of the Gospel* 2013).

A key to the newness of this moment lies in the challenge presented to every disciple to contextualise the Gospel in the real situation of today's world and the lives of the poor, and in responding to the joy of the Gospel, to engage in transforming mission. Pope Francis writes:

> I dream of a missionary option, that is a missionary impulse capable of transforming everything. (#27).

All are called to accept Christ and his Gospel and to become missionary disciples. Pope Francis also calls for a poor Church that is also a Church of the poor. The prophetic nature of missional work in the postmodern era has been clearly set out in this initial manifesto.

Laudato Si' (*Care for Our Common Home* 2015) is a truly prophetic document because it pictures a future which is a transformation of the present. Francis sees nature as a gift to all, and all as a part of nature. He critiques the misuse of power and self-centred approaches to 'progress', and calls for a simpler lifestyle. *Laudato Si* (LS)'s assumptions about the human and the nature and demands of justice today are very challenging,

In his latest document *Gaudete et Exsultate* (2018) Pope Francis reminds Catholics that all are called to holiness in and through their commitment to God's mission in Jesus. The nature of this commitment has already been spelled out by Pope Francis and he continues to do in his witness and his teaching, and in his insistence on dialogue.

Reflect and Discuss

Because Catholics belong to a worldwide community of communities, the missional insights generated by one group, in a particular time and place, flow to another and inspire that group's own quest for faithfulness to the mission of Jesus. This process of growth in missional wisdom is ongoing in the life of the Church and has been a strong feature in recent decades. It is given leadership through the work of synods and when popes exercise their teaching role.

1. How does our community come to understand and celebrate its own missional journey, one which others before us have started, and which we continue in our time and place?

2. How can Australian schools more effectively support one another in generating missional insight and commitment?

CHAPTER 8
Dialogue – a Vital Mode of Mission

Each member of the faithful and all Christian communities are called to practise dialogue, although not always to the same degree or in the same way. The contribution of the laity is indispensable in his area … (Pope John Paul II Redemptoris Missio #57).

'Dialogue' is one of the most important elements of mission today, although it is not always well understood. This central importance has led to the inclusion of a chapter devoted specifically both to dialogue and to aspects of its emergence in the Christian journey in our time.

Many people associate dialogue fairly exclusively with inter-religious dialogue, which is a vital area of dialogue, so much so that many excellent initiatives have been taken at a range of levels across the country under the auspices of various Church institutions – universities, schools, parishes, religious orders. This has occurred in response to our religiously plural context and the challenges this presents to humans living together productively and in peace. However, dialogue is a broad and deep concept, one that is central to what it means to be human, to make meaning, to learn, and to live with others. Its importance in all areas of human living can scarcely be over-estimated.

'Dialogue' entered the Catholic lexicon in the 1960s when, in setting out the agenda for his papacy, the newly elected Pope Paul VI, called for the Church to 'enter into dialogue with the modern world'. The call came in his first encyclical entitled *Ecclesiam Suam* (1964). At the time bishops from around the world were assembled for the Second Vatican Council II (1962-5). Pope John XXIII, who inaugurated the Council, had died and Paul VI was elected his successor.

A principal item of business for the Council was the *identity of the Church*. As we have already discussed, mission and identity are integral to one another. So conversations about mission, identity and dialogue became closely intertwined in the work of the Council, and set the foundations for the life of the Church from that time onwards.[22]

At more or less the same time, Western philosophers were exploring the nature of language and the role it plays in the formation of human identity. By 'language' they meant the way words, gestures and symbols are used to convey meaning. In their discussions, 'dialogue' emerged as being constitutive of who we are as human beings. Theologians drew on this philosophical work as they sought a deeper understanding of mission in the world today.

Dialogue Constructs Human Identity

As humans, we have an innate capacity to search for and choose the right word, gesture or symbol, when we wish to communicate. For example, when I am mad about something, I know that 'mad' is the right choice of word to convey how I am feeling. Similarly, when I see a car driving by, I know that 'car', rather than 'horse' or 'motor-bike', is the right word to describe the object I see moving by. Philosophers call this capacity to choose the right word '*intrinsic rightness*'.[23] It is a human characteristic that we take for granted, but one that distinguishes us from other animals.

In using language we are constantly making choices about words, gestures and symbols in terms of what is right and what is good, and such choices come to encode what we value. The choices we make reveal us both to ourselves and to others. In many cases when we enter into conversation with another person, we not only learn something about that person, we also learn something about ourselves. This process of mutual learning distinguishes dialogue from other types of 'speech event'.

Dialogue is a special form of speech event in which important insights emerge about how we see the world and the stance we take to it, and how the other sees the world and his or her stance to it. **The result is mutual learning**.

Authentic dialogue must meet two basic conditions:

- Recognition that we see the world from a particular perspective and this leads us to take a particular stance towards it. Recognition that the other is similarly placed, and that we are willing to establish what his or her view or stance is, and to face up to the questions this raises for us.

- We are willing to make the imaginative leap necessary to understand the world from within the other's worldview and stance.

In learning about the perspective and stance of the other, including why he or she uses language the way they do, we also learn what they value. This can present a very real challenge to how we see the world.

In dialogue, therefore, we not only learn about the world of the other, we learn something about how we define ourselves. Dialogue often challenges what we have been brought up to take as 'normal' by raising questions that challenge our self-understanding, but only if we are prepared to listen carefully.

Dialogue with God

'Dialogue' is an appropriate word to choose in describing humanity's relationship with God. Just as we see the world from a particular perspective and stance, so too does God. God helps us understand something of this perspective via the scriptures, pre-eminently in the teaching, mission, life, death and resurrection of Jesus, in prayer, and in life within the faith community.

There is a problem, however, in articulating God's perspective, because it comes to us enmeshed in a web of human language and is further restricted by our capacity to makes sense of this web.

Jesus used words, gestures, and symbols to convey God's view of the world. Often he taught in paradoxical ways that challenged his listeners to think things through for themselves. Across human history, Church leaders have endeavoured to resolve these paradoxes and present Christian faith in propositional form. While done with the best of intentions, and deemed necessary in difficult circumstances of confusion and conflict, this approach can mask the fundamentally dialogical nature of God's revelation. It can conceal the Christian community's task of interpreting the meaning of what God has revealed, especially at times when historical and cultural contexts change. Added to this, Christians have to deal with the consequences of earlier attempts to understand what

God has revealed, including attempts to reduce this to a set of propositions.

Against this background, we understand Jesus as God's Word disclosing how God sees the world, and challenging us to make the imaginative leap into God's view of things, comparing it with our own construction. In this process we learn something, not only about God's intentions for humankind, but also a good deal about ourselves and the faith community to which we belong. This self-defining form of dialogue finds fruitful expression in individual and communal prayer and in missional commitment.

Dialogue with the World = Mission

When recent popes have called for 'dialogue with the world', they have been talking about the willingness of Christians to take the life experiences of their contemporaries seriously. They have been acknowledging God's Spirit at work in the world, effecting God's intentions for humanity. They have also been asking the faith communities to read the 'signs of the times' (Matt 16:2-3).

If Christians wish to make the world a better place, they cannot do this on their own; they need to work with other people of good will, Christian and other than Christian. Just as God chooses to dialogue with Christians through Jesus, so we need to dialogue with others in continuing the works that Jesus initiated. This means being able to understand the world from their stance and point of view, and to access the positives in this so that it then becomes possible to work together and establish the rapport needed to make deeper engagement possible.

Dialogue of this type often demands an initial suspension of judgement about what we take as 'normal'. This is the pre-condition for working together on common projects, despite serious differences. In technical terms this engagement in common projects is referred to as *the dialogue of action (activities)*, a phrase used by Pope John Paul II in his teaching on mission (*Redemptoris Missio*, #57). A spectacular example of this form of dialogue is the collaboration in different parts of the world between religious sisters and others with sections of the sex industry, working together to stamp out the sexual slavery of migrant and refugee women.

Mission as Prophetic Dialogue

The mission of Jesus, particularly on behalf of the marginalised in society, involves both partnership and prophecy. Those who hold power, and particularly if they profit personally by their position, are seldom open to challenge on behalf of the powerless, and those doing so can expect opposition, even danger. Consequently, there is always need for prophetic action by advocacy, confrontation, action, and well-articulated submissions.

These kinds of action, if they are to be effective, call for dialogue among those undertaking them, so as to enable a strong and concerted stance. At times, too, articulation of the hope that keeps Christians committed to such action on behalf of the marginalised must occur not only for their own sake, but also for those who, bemused, ask why they bother. The following passage from 1 Peter 3:15 has become one of the great mission texts of our time:

> Always be ready to make your defence to anyone who demands from you an accounting for the hope that is in you; yet do it with gentleness and reverence.

In summary, dialogue plays a key role in the relationships by which we come to define who we are and who we want to become. At a communal level, it enables members of a faith-based group to negotiate a common understanding of what they value and therefore of how they can work together to achieve a common purpose. This inevitably leads to the search for dialogue partners beyond the group.

As they make this journey, community members not only come to understand their partners better, but come to a deeper understanding of their own identity as Christian. They engage in their project with the assurance that God's Spirit is at work not only in the Church, but also in the wider world as well. This realisation engenders confidence that there will always be dialogue partners to be found in achieving God's mission.

The points made so far about dialogue become concrete in many areas of school life, not least that of inter-religious dialogue. For example, many schools across Australia are currently implementing the *Enhancing Catholic School Identity* (ECSI) project. In ECSI the role of the teacher is interpreted as witness, expert (in things Catholic), and moderator of dialogue among students whose outlooks are shaped by a Christian worldview, a worldview of another faith, or other worldview. As moderator of dialogue the teacher needs to understand what authentic dialogue involves and be well practiced in the process. An assumption of the ECSI model is that, through dialogue, students come to a better understanding of their own religious and cultural identities. As this happens with students, it has a flow-on effect for teachers and others in the school community.

Dialogue is a mode of learning that is essential to identity formation and, while ECSI focuses attention on its importance in the Religious Education classroom, it has much wider application in teaching and learning.[24] We see, following our Reflection and Discussion, an example of the dialogue of life occurring through daily life and some respectful and enjoyable initiatives undertaken within a local community. As many such initiatives characterise our schools, this example could be multiplied across the states and territories. Can your community recognise the challenge of God's mission presented by our changing society, and take an 'imaginative leap' in the face of the privilege of pluralism?

Reflection

Catholics have a range of ideas about dialogue. Those who interpret the Catholic faith tradition simply in propositional terms see little value in dialogue. Those who interpret it in terms of God's mission, and have an awareness of the Holy Spirit at work in history and cultures, see dialogue as central to discipleship. There is ongoing tension among Church members and leaders about these two approaches to dialogue, and a number of intermediate positions exist.

1. In your understanding and experience, how does the tension arising from the two approaches to faith identified here surface in the life of the Church community?

2. How is it best dealt with in school life, including in the classroom?

Mission as Inculturation, Witness and Dialogue
St Patrick's, Stawell

Guided Learning Walks in Religious Education provide a catalyst for inculturation and an invitation to dialogue between students, teachers and parents at St Patrick's School Stawell. In planning for the walks, teachers prepare a Godly Play lesson that might have particular resonance for parents who are seeking to engage in conversations about faith and belief with their children. The facilitator of the learning walks briefs parents about what they might see and should listen for prior to entering the classroom. Equipped with iPads, parents then observe teachers and children interacting in the lesson and take photos of the activity.

In the circle time afterwards, parents share what they have observed, how the teacher witnesses to faith with the children and how the children's life experiences and wonderings about faith are drawn into the dialogue. They see that children naturally connect life and faith and that children are constantly seeking to make meaning. In evaluating the approach, parents indicate that the guided learning walks have allowed them to see their children and the living faith tradition in a way that makes sense in contemporary culture. When, to use the words of Jesus' invitation to his potential disciples in John 1:38-39, parents 'come and see' how their children talk about their faith, that classroom experience opens up the possibility of continued dialogue about life and faith at home.

For teachers, the learning walks have brought increased understanding of the privileged place of dialogue in the classroom and the importance of witnessing to their faith with children and parents. The experience of inviting children (and parents) into a place of encounter with Jesus speaks to all in their school community.

... the classroom experience opens up the possibility of continued dialogue about life and faith at home.

CHAPTER 9

Mission – the Task of the Whole Community

Each Christian and every community must discern the path that the Lord points out, but all of us are asked to obey his call to go forth from our own comfort zone in order to reach all the 'peripheries' in need of the light of the Gospel. (Pope Francis The Joy of the Gospel #20).

We each have at best a partial grasp of our faith tradition conditioned by such factors as our early introduction to it, education, life history, and experiences of being part of a faith community. Each of us views the reality of faith from a particular and limited perspective.

Well-known U.S. Catholic authors Evelyn and James Whitehead offer an important insight in noting that in matters of faith no one believes it all, and no one believes it all the time because this is the task and responsibility of the whole Christian faith community. The Whiteheads suggest that, this being the case, we need to 'befriend' our faith tradition in much the same way as we do our cultural tradition. By this they mean that we do not expect our friends to be perfect. We accept them for who they are, warts and all, because we think they are worth knowing and that their real value will be revealed more fully over time.

Something similar can be said of a group's mission. No group does it all, and no one group committed to a specific form of mission, such as prayer and worship or justice and peace, does it all the time. It is the mission of the whole Christian community to make the Kingdom of God present in human history, now and across time. Mission, understood in this sense has a never-ending story. Secondly, this story is inclusive and involves those outside the community as well as the community's members.

As an example, as we noted in Chapter Five, the bishops at Vatican II developed a formal document on Christian education. One of the 12 principles they enunciated was the Church's commitment to the right of all young people to an education. In pursuing this aspect of the Church's mission, the Christian Brothers are partnering with the Franciscans and the United Nations at the latter's Geneva Headquarters. The working group's task is to systematically review U.N. members' records of honouring children's right to an education, and to recommend changes where this right is not being honoured, particularly for young people who are marginalised.

In today's complex world, when it comes to mission 'no one does it all'. Every group committed to mission needs dialogue partners to be effective. Most people know this intuitively and feel excluded when they should be, but are not, included. This can be the situation of parents in Catholic schools and of young people in parishes.

Mission Exists in the Concrete and Addresses Important Human Needs

Mission does not exist in the abstract; it involves concrete actions demanded by important human needs generated within a particular context. Mission requires an interpretation of the context and an identification of emerging needs. In Jesus' language it requires leaders to 'read the signs of the times' (Matt 16:2-3).

The human needs to which mission is a response can exist at several levels. At the physical level mission can mean helping those who lack food, are homeless, cannot pay their rent, need accommodation and employment, or are refugees in search of a safe and secure country in which to live. At the socio-cultural level it can mean educating young people, or helping migrant parents figure out how the Australian 'system' works. It can equally mean gearing education programs to the needs of people who are marginalised by their home circumstances or in terms of their natural ability. For leaders, it can mean building community in an increasingly individualised popular culture. At the spiritual level, it means helping people in their search for meaning and coherence in making sense of and finding purpose in their lives. It means providing meaningful opportunities for prayer and worship, and creating liturgies that inspire and nourish people.

While important human needs manifest themselves in particular human contexts, they tend to vary when an era changes. As a consequence, mission can become something of a 'moveable feast' that needs to be closely monitored; it is not always well tracked by 'mission statements'.

While there are cultural and social organisations (government and non-government) that address people's physical and social needs, there is not the same attention paid to people's spiritual and religious needs. Indeed, many people, including students, do not recognise that they have such needs. This is the situation that teachers in Catholic schools struggle to come to grips with both personally and educationally, and so is an important aspect of the school's present mission context.

Faith as Integral to Life's Journey

Today, faith is understood as an important part of the journey we make throughout life. For many Catholics its importance seems to wax and wane as their lives continue to unfold. As we make the journey and as our circumstances and the context in which we live change, we are constantly forced to rethink and re-evaluate what at an earlier period we took as 'normal'. This includes what we believe, and the way we believe.

For many people this situation involves a great deal of angst that is often more than they can tolerate. It leads to a range of escapist behaviours that can be physically harmful and psychologically and spiritually debilitating, creating a range of human needs particular to our cultural situation. Teachers in Catholic schools are not immune from the dilemmas of contemporary living.

In an earlier era, Catholics tended to look to Church leaders and Church teaching to provide an interpretive framework and also a guide on questions such as: what to believe, what to value, what was right, and how to feel. Up until the 1970s Catholic teaching and practices were accepted as defining what was 'normal', so the Church and its clergy were accorded generally unchallenged interpretive authority in determining how Catholics made sense of their lives. Not any more! A number of major research projects conducted here and in the US make it clear that the majority of Catholics formulate their answers to the above questions on the basis of their personal interpretive authority rather than the Church's teaching or authority. This is not to say that they ignore the latter, but that it no longer carries the weight that it once did.

This relatively recent development is part of what philosophers such a Lyotard call 'the postmodern condition'. It is a cultural malaise that leaves many people feeling isolated and anxious in their individualised world without any fixed frame of reference in knowing what to believe, what to value, how to feel, what is right, or even how to behave since they have no way of determining what can be taken as 'normal' any more. The postmodern condition provides the contemporary mission context for Catholic educators.

The question for many discerning Catholic educators is this: How to understand and address the contemporary mission context and the needs emerging from it? In the balance of this chapter we suggest an approach that we have found helpful. We begin by returning to the notion that mission has both *modes and forms*. As was noted in Chapter Six, mission can take many forms, as there is no single way to make the Kingdom of God present in people's lives. There are multiple significant human needs and multiple ways in which these can be addressed. Secondly, mission is best understood as the responsibility of a group because of the power groups have to amplify the capacity of individuals. Teachers are well aware of how this dynamic works out in schools.

Forms and Modes of Mission

The forms of mission are responses people make to areas of human life that generate concrete human needs. In this context, people endeavour to live out the call of the Gospel in service to others. The forms of mission bring focus and assign priority to the ways in which a group responds to needs in the service of the Gospel. Each form of mission has both a 'what' and a 'why'.

It goes without saying that the focus and priorities of a school will generally be different in important ways from those of a parish, even though they share the same 'why'.

The *modes of mission* are the essential activities associated with any particular form that mission takes. There are three modes of mission:

- proclamation by word (Word) – the message or the why – that links service of others to the call of the Gospel

- proclamation by witness (Witness) – the what – providing a specific service to others

- dialogue – the how (Dialogue) – engaging with partners with whom it is necessary to collaborate in meeting deep human needs. (Dialogue includes creating the conditions in which collaboration becomes possible.)

In reviewing its mission emphases, a school should be able to answer the following three questions:

- *How can our efforts to create Kingdom spaces in the lives of our students be interpreted as carrying on the mission of Jesus?* (Witness value)

- *How do we explain to others why what we do is important in carrying on the mission of Jesus?* (Word value)

- *Who are, or should be, our dialogue partners in this endeavour and how do we engage with them?* (Dialogue value)

Mission Matrix: Making Mission Real

As we saw in Chapter Six, the forms and modes of mission can be brought together to form a matrix. The forms of mission in the matrix are those current in the Church's official teaching.

The matrix makes it clear that faith-based organisations will differ in the emphasis they give to the different forms that mission can take. Similarly, with any particular form of mission, different emphases will be put on the relative importance accorded to Witness, Word and Dialogue. As already noted, the emphasis in schools differs from that in parishes. In the former, dialogue is now seen as an essential tool in learning. In parishes dialogue is commonly, if at times unfairly, viewed as 'missing in action'.

Most schools now engage in some social justice activities. However research consistently shows that, while the emphasis is on Witness (the What), students do not always understand the Why of what they do. Nor are they usually able to articulate the connection between their faith tradition and what they are undertaking as practical action.

The Mission Matrix: A Vigilance Grid

The final reflective exercise brings together various themes explored in this Guide. It asks you to create a mission profile for your school, then to do the same for the parish(es) associated with the school, to compare the results, to see what can be learned about mission, and how the way mission is understood and engaged in relates to context and important human needs.

For this exercise you will need two copies of the mission matrix reproduced below. Using the first copy:

Exercise

1. Assign a rating out of 10 for the relative importance of EACH form of mission as it is pursued in your school. Add up the grand total.

2. As a separate exercise, assign a rating out of 5 for the relative importance of Witness Word and Dialogue for each of the forms of mission acknowledged in section 1 above. Add up the totals for Witness, Word and Dialogue.

3. Repeat this exercise using the second copy of the matrix for the parish associated with your school.

Discussion

Discuss the following questions:

1. What do the ratings given to the forms of mission tell you about the way needs are assessed (a) in your school (b) in the parish?

	MODES OF MISSION		
	Proclamation		
Forms of Mission	by Word	by Witness	through Dialogue
Pastoral Ministry			
Prayer and Liturgy			
Defence of Human Rights			
Inculturation			
Liberation			
Justice and Peace			
Reconciliation			
Human Development			
Inter-religious Dialogue			
Care for the Earth			
Other			
Totals			

Mission in the Postmodern Era

2. What do the ratings on the modes of mission tell you about their relative importance in the way (a) the school (b) the parish engages in mission?

Analysis

1. What sense do you make of these results?

2. What conclusions can you draw from these results about how the school's mission is formulated and how it is pursued?

3. What conclusions can you draw from the results about how the parish's mission in formulated and how it is pursued?

The question for many thinking Catholic educators is this: How to understand and address the emerging mission context and the needs emerging from it?

Mission as Social Justice, Reconciliation and Dialogue – St Alipius, Ballarat East

The ten percent of students at St Alipius' School Ballarat East, who identify as Aboriginal or Torres Strait Islander, claim their aboriginality with pride in a school community that recognises, affirms and proclaims the inherent dignity of every person. The school has a deep commitment to exploring Catholic identity and the way in which the Catholic tradition, recognising all as children of God, calls all people into community, respect and solidarity. This commitment takes on a particular meaning when viewed as a journey of reconciliation and through the lens of dialogue with the culture and traditions of Aboriginal students and their families.

St Alipius' School has moved away from a token indigenous curriculum unit to embed Aboriginal perspectives across the curriculum. This is actively supported by the local Aboriginal community and enhanced by the honest feedback of Aboriginal parents, who are genuine dialogue partners to school leaders. The stories, spirituality and culture of Aboriginal students are shared, celebrated and affirmed. The principles of Catholic social teaching and Catholic sacramental theology provide inspiration for the witness of school leaders to journey together, to build relationships, and to grow in mutual understanding. This approach both ensures that the school teaches Aboriginal children respectfully and that all children are able to recognise a range of perspectives (including an Aboriginal one) as they encounter and make sense of the world.

CHAPTER 10
Theological Reflection for Mission

'Doing theology', or the art of theological reflection, is a grass-roots process of religious meaning-making. It seeks to bring together human experience, faith and culture, in dealing with important issues that lie at the core of mission. Theological reflection is an art rather than a science in that it requires discernment and judgment.

In engaging in theological reflection, we need to consider both a model and a process. The model identifies the essential elements that need to be brought together so that the process chosen leads to meaningful outcomes. While a model can give rise to a number of processes, in this Guide we will focus on one consolidated process that has proved its value.

Criteria for a sound model

A sound model of theological reflection needs to respect the nature of the meaning-making process, and the human experience of the people involved.

In their seminal study, *Method in Ministry*, James and Evelyn Whitehead present a model that meets these criteria.[25] The model is set out in the diagram below. Our model indicates that, in looking at an issue of concern, any useful process of theological reflection will first acknowledge the human experience of the people involved. Secondly, it will seek to access the wisdom of the faith tradition – what light does the Bible, and especially the gospels, throw on the situation? Thirdly, it will also explore what the knowledge base of our culture has to say: are there sociological, scientific, historical, anthropological, literary, artistic, or other issues being played out here that we need to consider?

A consolidated method

The method outlined is an adaptation of the **See Judge Act** process that has a long history in Catholic Action where it has proved both accessible and very helpful, not least in the formation of young people. It is associated with the Belgian Cardinal Joseph Cardijn (d 1967) and the Young Christian Workers (YCW). The **See Judge Act** method is here complemented by the work of others – the Whiteheads, Patricia O'Connell-Killen with her colleague John De Beer,[26] and Richard Osmer.[27] When Cardijn developed **See Judge Act** he assumed that people had a certain grasp of their faith tradition. However, in our de-traditionalised world we can no longer assume any such thing; a more sophisticated approach is now called for.

In the original **See Judge Act** method the emphasis was on applying faith to life. This is good as far as it goes. However, many models ignore the role culture plays in how people make sense of life, and this is a serious deficiency. Culture is always the default frame of reference in meaning-making unless some other frame of reference is explicitly brought into play.

Theological reflection invites us to acknowledge this, and to critique its adequacy as a starting point. It does this by exploring the wisdom of our faith tradition. However, our faith tradition also has its limitations. As held in human communities it inevitably contains biases that are cultural in origin, since the faith of an individual or community always develops within a culture and can be expressed only through the medium of culture.

The dialogue between faith and culture therefore needs to be two-way and when it occurs, both the faith tradition and the cultural tradition benefit: theological reflection opens up the possibility that understanding of faith can be enriched, and also that culture can be improved (evangelised) as human concerns are addressed.

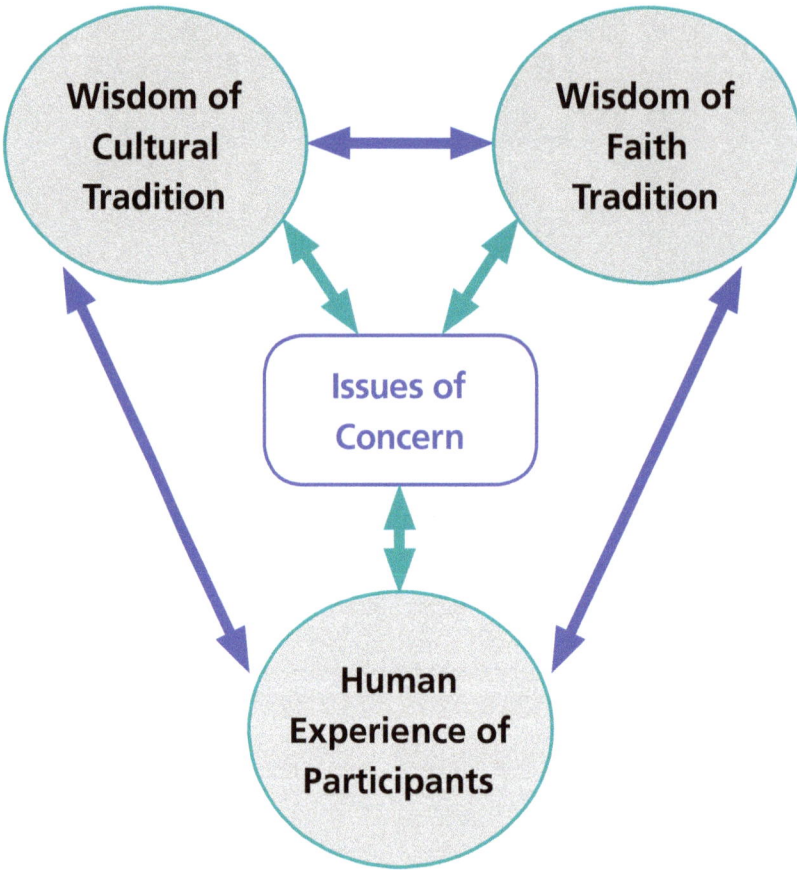

Whitehead & Whitehead Method in Ministry

Developing a composite process of 'doing theology'

Drawing on the work of Osmer, the basic framework given below breaks the process into 'moments'. Added to Osmer's framework is the 'focusing moment' which is pivotal in the work of O'Connell Killen and de Beer.

Each of the six 'moments' has a defining question.

Let's Get Practical

At this point readers are invited to begin consideration of a particular mission issue. The issue selected here, by way of example, is the missional imperative, so clearly identified by Pope Francis, to care for the earth, our common home.

How can this community better care for the earth, our common home, and do so as an expression of our Christian faith?

See, Judge, Act Process

See

▲ Step 1 **The Descriptive Moment**
What is going on here?

▲ Step 2 **The Interpretive Moment**
Why is it going on?

Judge

▲ Step 3 **The Evaluative Moment**
What is the preferred future we want to achieve?

▲ Step 4 **The Focusing Moment**
What precisely do we need to respond to?

Act

▲ Step 5 **The Response Moment**
What actions/steps do we now need to take?

▲ Step 6 **The Review Moment**
How effective has our response been?

See

▲ **Step 1** The Descriptive Moment
What is going on here?

- **Comment:** In this pre-critical stage, the aim is to describe the situation, including the feelings generated among the participants. This should be done in non-judgmental terms.

Process
Look at the situation and describe its key features.

- Where have participants seen harm inflicted on Mother Earth?
- What are they doing as a community to care for the earth?
- Who is doing what? How do people react to this?
- What have they achieved to date?

▲ **Step 2** The interpretive moment
(Why is it going on?)

Comment: This is the *critical stage* in which life culture and faith have to be brought into dialogue so that the group makes meaning from what is happening, and articulates this. The group will tend at first to draw on secular sources, because our primary frame of reference in making sense of life in our culture is secular.

Step 2 seeks to surface this initial bias and to critique it, at first with reference to what else the culture might have to offer.

It then brings faith into play *as a qualifying factor*. The wisdom of our faith tradition has something more or different to offer that may be helpful. This creates the possibility of dialogue between faith and culture in making sense of human situations.

There are many good works such as action for justice and peace and care for our common home that even those Christians committed to them, may not see as expressions of faith; they remain simply 'good works' in a separate basket from matters of faith. Theological reflection aims to integrate them in a person's or group's Christian worldview.

Process
Exploring frameworks of interpretation

- *How do participants best explain people's motivation in dealing with care for the earth issues?*
- *What role (if any) does their faith tradition play in making sense of initiatives currently underway?*

You can invite the community to consider the core Biblical relationships between humans and God, humans with one another, and humans with the natural world. Which relationships are being compromised by the current situation of the earth?

Think about Jesus' metaphor of the kingdom of God. What would the situation be if the community were truly a 'kingdom space' in regard to care for the earth?

Or again, bearing in mind how the lack of care for the earth has resulted in extreme poverty, put the great Biblical question: who is being marginalised in this situation? Worldwide? Locally? How? Why? Where are faith and culture aligned/misaligned in the way the situation is being interpreted?

Judge

▲ Step 3 The evaluative moment
(What is the preferred future that we should strive to achieve?

Comment: In Step 3 the aim is to bring imagination and feeling into the reflection so that the process can move from the head to the heart.

The genius of Jesus' Kingdom of God motif is that it remains a permanent challenge to the human imagination. Participants are prompted to be aware that their best efforts are always provisional. There is always more to be imagined.

Process
Brainstorm possible solutions set within norms drawn from culture and faith.

Consider the following questions:

- *What does the group see as a preferred future in addressing care for the earth? (Let imagination come into play.)*

> *The dialogue between faith and culture needs to be two-way and, when it occurs, both the faith tradition and the cultural tradition benefit...*

- *What norms sourced in faith and/or culture are being implied in the way they imagine this future?*
- *How do criteria drawn from faith and culture align/misalign with each other in deciding what the preferred future should be?*

▲ Step 4 The focusing moment
(What precisely do we need to respond to?)

Comment: Any process of theological reflection involves discernment, a sorting out of the essential from the non-essential. O'Connell-Killen and De Beer call this getting to 'the heart of the matter'. They point out that there are a number of ways of approaching the task that involve right-brain techniques. For example, if no solution immediately suggests itself, the facilitator asks people to sit with the problem till insight emerges, put the problem before God in prayer, and perhaps, if necessary, seek advice from outside the group.

Prayer has a vital place in theological reflection. It gives leaders the confidence to trust their intuition in discerning what lies at the heart of complex issues.

It is important to note that there is no 'right' answer as to the heart of the matter. A community or group arrives at a provisional solution, the 'heart of the matter' for now.

Theological reflection is an ongoing journey of interpretation and meaning-making. As the group goes further they may come to other aspects of this issue and work with it more broadly or deeply, but in due course.

Having discerned what the heart of the matter is at least at this stage, it is important also to discern the first step in addressing it. Sometimes this involves estimating people's readiness to respond. Awareness-raising about the importance of an issue may be the first step in addressing it.

Process
Community discernment

Consider the following questions:

- *What seem to be emerging as the key issues?*
- *What is the first step in formulating a response?*
- *Does the situation warrant direct action or are there readiness factors that need to be addressed? What are they?*

Copyright Columban Centre for Christian-Muslim Relations

Act

▲ **Step 5** The response moment
(What does the community need to do? How can they move from head and heart through to hands and feet?)

Comment: The aim in this step is to identify how to proceed in order to arrive at the 'preferred future'. This is the future the community can only partly imagine, but with the glimpses available to them, they can go forward, knowing that together, in prayerful joy and collaboration with the Holy Spirit, they can contribute to a better future.

Process
Planning as a community.

- What is the plan to raise awareness (if necessary) about the need for action?
- Who needs to be involved?
- What action will be taken?
- How will it be planned? Implemented?
- What resourcing will be required?
- Who needs to be involved? When? How?

▲ **Step 6** The Review Moment
(How effective has the response been?)

Comment: All interventions have outcomes (some good, some bad; some expected, some unexpected). These need to be assessed in the light of original intentions. Reviewing the outcomes may throw up further areas of concern to be pursued.

Process
Review how the plan was developed, adopted and implemented

Consider the following questions:

- *What outcomes did the work of awareness-raising achieve?*
- *In what ways have these outcomes moved the community towards the preferred future? In what ways has this become more achievable? More elusive? Why?*
- *Did the participants' discernment of the heart of the matter prove accurate?*
- *What assumptions (unstated) did they make that have not proved viable?*

The final step leads back to the first, particularly when, as is usually the case, the response does not lead in one attempt to the outcome that people had initially hoped for. The method is a form of *praxis* that may run over several cycles, proceeding like a spiral, until the preferred future, or some re-negotiated form of it, is achieved.

Conclusion
God's Mission Has a Faith Community

The story of mission is that of people feeling called to form a community so as to continue God's mission as they know it in the mission of Jesus. At its best, mission continues in our time in the form of good news to the poor and marginalised, to those who are truth-seekers, to those who search for meaning in their lives, and to suffering Mother Earth, whose degradation cries out for redress.

In our Catholic communities, slowly and surely we are beginning to reflect anew on the breadth and depth of God's mission, and to become intentionally involved in a 'new creation', or to use Jesus' chosen image, God's kingdom. This 'kingdom' bears no resemblance whatsoever to earthly kingdoms. Indeed, Jesus went out of his way to make it very clear that God's Kingdom is the reverse of the values and practices of many earthly realms. It is a place for honouring and valuing people and Mother Earth through practical and humble service. It is a place of equality, discernment and dialogue in the pursuit of love, justice and reconciliation.

This *Educator's Guide to Mission in Practice* features a sample of real-life efforts which educating communities in every diocese will be able to recognise as practical, generous and helpful, as they go about shaping their responses to the challenges of God's mission in their own contexts.

God's mission has a multitude of school communities at its service. The potential for good in our world is enormous, not only in an immediate sense, but in the future, where young people, already formed in reflective involvement during their schooling, will be well prepared to continue God's mission in homes, workplaces, and social settings across the world.

Just as was the case in Jesus' time, the Kingdom of God remains a permanent challenge to human imagination. Indeed, the possibilities for renewal and goodness in our world are limited only by our imaginal horizons and capacities for commitment. So let's push out those horizons, joyfully develop those capacities, and join together in mission!

Prayer

The Our Father

Our Father,
who art in heaven,
hallowed be thy name;
Thy kingdom come;
Thy will be done on earth as in heaven.
Give us this day our daily bread;
and forgive us our trespasses
as we forgive those who trespass against us;
and lead us not into temptation,
but deliver us from evil.
Amen

Prayer to Mary by Pope Francis

...Star of the new evangelisation,
help us to bear radiant witness to communion,
service, ardent and generous faith,
justice and love of the poor,
that the joy of the Gospel
may reach to the ends of the earth,
illuminating even the fringes of our world.

Mother of the living Gospel,
wellspring of happiness for God's little ones,
pray for us.

Amen. Alleluia!

The Magnificat

(Taken from Luke 1:46-55)

My soul magnifies the Lord

And my spirit rejoices in God my Savior;

Because He has regarded the lowliness of His handmaid;

For behold, henceforth all generations shall call me blessed;

Because He who is mighty has done great things for me,

and holy is His name;

And His mercy is from generation to generation

on those who fear Him.

He has shown might with His arm,

He has scattered the proud in the conceit of their heart.

He has put down the mighty from their thrones,

and has exalted the lowly.

He has filled the hungry with good things,

and the rich He has sent away empty.

He has given help to Israel, his servant, mindful of His mercy

Even as he spoke to our fathers, to Abraham and to his posterity forever.

Endnotes

1. Matthew used 'kingdom of heaven' out of sensitivity for his predominantly Jewish community.

2. Chapter 2 in the encyclical *Redemptoris Missio*, 1991.

3. Throughout this Guide the words 'missionary' and 'missional' are used interchangeably. The former, though widely used, may convey limiting connotations for some people. Hence the simple adjective 'missional' is gaining currency.

4. The work of Anthony Gittins CSSp is acknowledged.

5. A helpful source in regard to discipleship is Donald Senior, *Jesus: A Gospel Portrait* (Mahwah: Paulist Press, 1992). The discussion in this chapter is indebted in part to the third chapter, 'Jesus and His Own', 51-61.

6. Ibid, 61.

7. NCEC A Framework for Formation for Mission, 2017. https://www.formationformission.com

8. For a summary of some of these see J & T. D'Orsa, *Catholic Curriculum: A Mission to the Heart of Young People* (Mulgrave: Garratt Publishing, 2011), chapter 5.

9. Gerald Arbuckle, *Catholic Identity or Identities* (Collegeville: The Liturgical Press, 2013).

10. Lieven Boeve, *God Interrupts History* (New York: Continuum, 2007).

11. The work of Lucien Legrand, *Unity and Plurality* (Maryknoll N.Y: Orbis, 1988) is acknowledged.

12. Legrand, 4.

13. A helpful discussion of the two creation traditions (the Priestly and the Yahwist) can be found in Walter Burghardt, *Justice: a Global Adventure* (Maryknoll N.Y: 2004), 16-17.

14. The work of Second Isaiah was composed during or after the Exile. It became attached to the manuscript of an earlier (8th century) prophet, but is now generally recognised as the work of a different prophet. Jesus quoted from Second Isaiah in the synagogue at Nazareth.

15. The seminal work of Senior and Stuhlmueller *The Biblical Foundations of Mission* (Maryknoll N.Y.: 1983) is acknowledged.

16. Pope Francis' Speech to the Students of Jesuit schools of Italy and Albania, quoted in Congregation for Catholic Education *Educating to Intercultural Dialogue in Catholic Schools: Living in Harmony for a Civilization of Love* (2013).

17. There had been no papal encyclical or similar document since *Divini Illius Magistri* of Pius XI in 1929.

18. Stephen Bevans & Roger Schroeder, *Constants in Context* (Maryknoll N.Y: Orbis, 2004), 86. Bevans and Schroeder are drawing on the work of Michael Green, *Evangelism in the Early Church* (Grand Rapids: Eerdmans, 1970), 173.

19. The work of mission anthropologist Louis Luzbetak has been very influential – *The Church and Cultures* (Maryknoll N.Y: Orbis, 1988).

20. A helpful treatment can be found in Chapter Seven 'A Single but Complex Reality' in Roger Schroeder, *What is the Mission of the Church?* (Maryknoll NY: Orbis, 2008), 112-127.

21. Readers are directed to the excellent and accessible publication *Bridges* produced by the Columban Centre for Christian-Muslim Relations, Blacktown. https://www.columban.org.au/about.../columban-centre-for-christian-muslim-relations...

22. Those who wish to study this further will find Australian scholar James McEvoy, *Leaving Christendom for Good: Church-World Dialogue in a Secular Age* (Lexington: Abington Books, 2014) a comprehensive treatment of aspects of the journey into dialogue.

23. Charles Taylor's theory of language can be accessed in McEvoy Part 2. ibid.

24. For a practical introduction to some concepts within this chapter see *Essentials of Dialogue: Guidance and activities for teaching and practising dialogue with young people*, which can be downloaded from the Tony Blair Institute for Global Change (https://institute.global) A valuable and accessible theological resource from the Federation of Asian Bishops' Conferences Office of Ecumenical and Inter-religious Affairs is Edmund Chia (ed) *Dialogue: Resource Manual for Catholics in Asia* (Bangkok: FABC-OEIA, 2001).

25. WHITEHEAD, James and Evelyn. *Method in Ministry: Theological Reflection and Christian Ministry* Revised edn (Kansas City: Sheed and Ward, 1995).

26. O'CONNELL KILLEN, Patricia and De BEER, John *The Art of Theological Reflection* (New York: Crossroad Publishing Company, 1994).

27. OSMER, Richard. *Practical Theology: An Introduction* (Grand Rapids: W. B. Eerdmans, 2008).

Further Reading

In moving more deeply into the Catholic experience of mission the following are recommended:

Roger Schroeder, *What is the Mission of the Church?: A Guide for Catholics*, (Maryknoll N.Y: Orbis, 2008)

Stephen Bevans and Roger Schroeder, *Constants in Context: A Theology of Mission for Today* (Maryknoll N.Y: Orbis, 2004). An encyclopaedic treatment of mission theology.

James and Evelyn Whitehead, *Community of Faith: Crafting Christian Communities Today* (Lincoln: iUniverse, 2001).

James Chukwuma Okoye *Israel and the Nations : A Mission Theology of the Old Testament* (Maryknoll N.Y:, Orbis, 2006)

The work emerging on mission from Christian sources other than Catholic is extensive and rewarding for the serious scholar of mission.

The Church's extensive corpus of recent magisterial documents on evangelising mission are downloadable from the Vatican website.

Other books in the Educator's Guide series

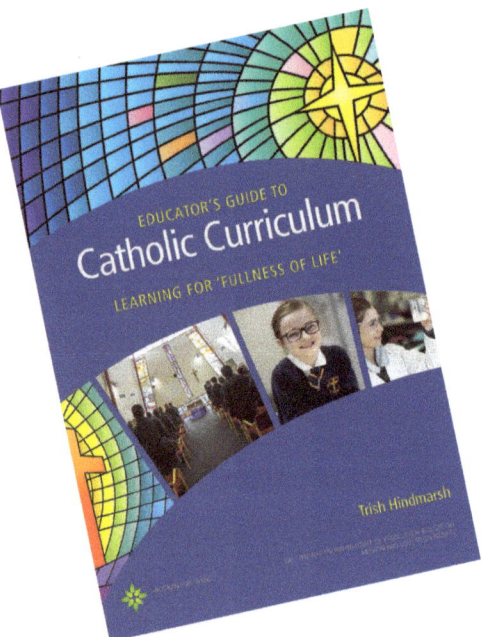

Educator's Guide to Catholic Curriculum

Learning for 'Fullness of Life'

by Patricia Hindmarsh

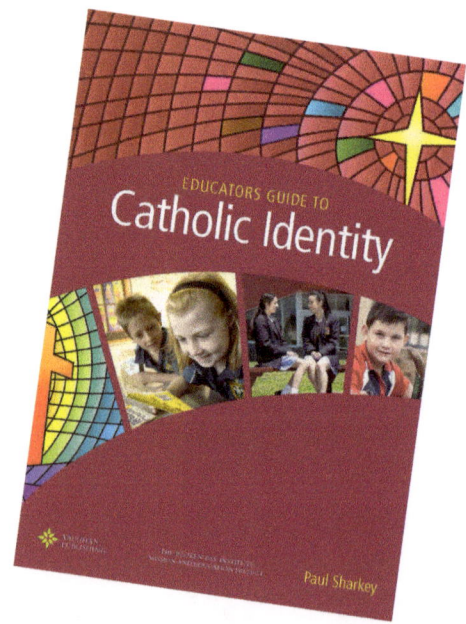

Educator's Guide to Catholic Identity

by Paul Sharkey

www.ingramcontent.com/pod-product-compliance
Lightning Source LLC
Chambersburg PA
CBHW042014170426
43195CB00046BA/2984

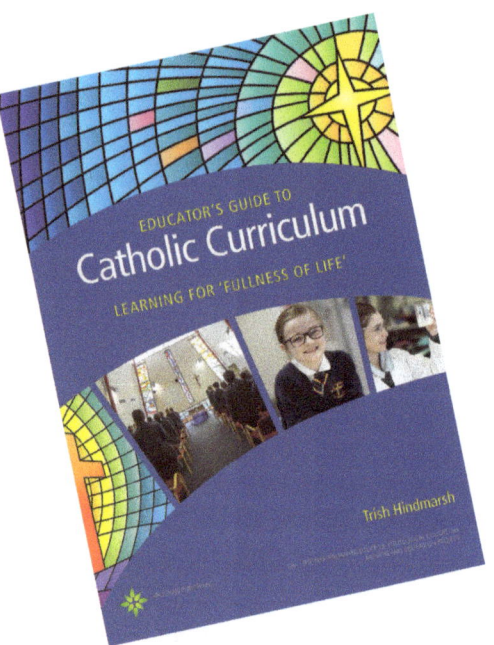

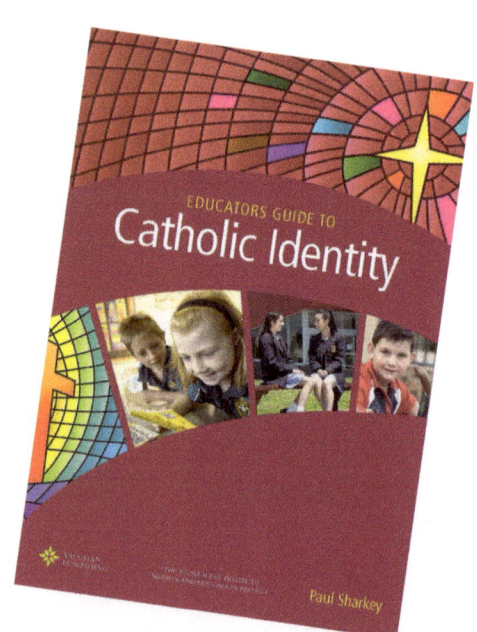